# *Know Yourself*

By Frank Mashaal and Hassan Elsebai

1

Dedication:

I would like to first give thanks to the Creator because without Him this book would not have been possible.

A family is the best gift the Creator can give us. This book is dedicated to my mom, Carolyn, my little brother, Knight, and my sister, Gabriella. I will cherish the time we spent together and will always dream about what could have been. This book is also dedicated to my father, Mohammed Mashaal, who passed away shortly before we began working on this book. Thank you for teaching me how to have "beautiful" patience, and the courage to give more. May the Most High grant you all mercy. Until we meet again.

I would like to thank my friend and coauthor, Hassan, for spending the last few years making this book come alive. I would like to thank my aunts and cousins. Thank you for being there through challenging times. I would like to thank my daughter, Evangelina, and my nephews, Ashton and Chance, for making me want to be a better role model. Finally, I would like to thank my brother, Mark, and his wife, Tjia. Thank you for always being there through life's ups and downs, for not judging me when I was in a low place, and for showing me tough love. As much as I have been through, you make me count my blessings and appreciate the life I have. Thank you.

Your son, brother, nephew, uncle, father, and cousin,

*Frank Mashaal*

# Table of Contents

# Introduction

One evening in Florence, Italy, some five centuries ago, history's greatest sculptor, Michelangelo, finished his famous statue of David. Bringing it into the town square in Florence, thousands flocked from adjacent cities and villages to see his masterpiece. The statue was a breathtaking sight. At twenty feet tall, the statue of the biblical character David astonished everyone in attendance and continues to astound anyone who visits it to this day.

One onlooker asked the artist, "Michelangelo, may God bless your hands; how did you create such a magnificent work of art?"

Michelangelo famously responded, "The sculpture is already complete within the marble block before I start my work. It is already there; I just have to chisel away the superfluous material."

Similarly, the best version of yourself is already within you. This book will guide your chisel to assist you in unveiling the masterpiece that already exists. All it takes to discover your best self is a steady hand, a vision, and a little bit of hard work.

…

It's easy to have faith when things are going well. It's easy to believe when the circumstances are right. But what about when all hell breaks loose? What happens when life puts you through harsh conditions forcing you to ascend out of pure darkness to save whatever is left of yourself? Hard times and trials are when belief is truly tested.

I have faced considerable suffering in life. I have experienced heartbreaking events beyond my control as well as misfortunes produced by my own manifestations and self-destruction. At thirteen years of age, I saw my mother, sister, and brother covered in blood. They lay dead before my eyes with bullets lodged in their skulls and faces. The trauma of losing my family wounded me deeply and in a way that left me with a chip on my shoulder living on my own at the age of fifteen.

My whole childhood seemingly ended overnight. I was forced to quickly grow up and become a man. I had my own apartment, and I was completely independent of any authority. I found myself racing through life without understanding why I was burdened with such great loss. I was misguided. I feared no consequences. The things I did tend to lead many to prison and leave many others dead. Feeling I had already lost everything, I was battling for my sanity by burying my memories and satiating my sorrow with dangerous drugs, wild parties, and even wilder women. My lifestyle was my escape—it allowed me to avoid confronting past trauma and the suffering that came with it.

I lived a crazy life, dealing drugs and running with gangs. The county jails seemed to have a revolving door for me. I got married just to get divorced a short while later, then watched another man step into my daughter's life.

Ill-gotten gains and illicit wealth eventually led to my destruction. A severe car crash left me disabled and needing multiple surgeries. I learned to walk a second time. During my lowest point, when I needed a friend, I had not one shoulder to lean on. I spent many Thanksgivings alone, staring out the window at the cold city streets and wondering, "Why me?" I struggled to overcome my old self, consisting of my old programming and bottled-up trauma buried deep inside. At thirty years old, I picked up the broken pieces and began the process of restarting my life. I died. At least the old version of me did.

If you are going through difficult times, I want you to realize that you have a powerful spirit and have the power to conquer anything you are determined to overcome. We can't control much of what transpires in life: Our loved ones will die, we will face disease and illness, be surprised with unexpected financial losses, and so on. We must face the reality that this world is overwhelmingly harsh.

As a participant in life, we will all experience many forms of sorrow and pain. However, the more adversity you overcome, the more strength and wisdom you will be blessed with to be a light for others. I wanted to write a book capable of elevating the minds of those who seek more from life. I wanted to write an inspirational book for those facing hardships or those who need inspiration and motivation to move beyond the depression or suffering they encounter.

This book will be a source of light and guidance enabling ascension from the depths. I truly know what it means to rise from the depths of hell and to overcome life's many challenges and begin to reprogram old behaviors and traumas that may hold us back from greatness and significance.

This book is a story about my life. It is a story of ups and downs and significant life changes. It is a story of how my life changed overnight after discovering my family had been murdered at the age of thirteen. It is a story of how I climbed the ranks of consciousness through egotistical thinking and was destroyed by my false desires. But this book is also a story of how I was completely destroyed and emerged from the depths of darkness to find the light that is the essence of us all. There is, after all, magnificence in pain when it pushes a person to face the darkness that lies within. Some people have more troubles than others; nonetheless, we all have a depth of hidden pain we choose to run from and cover up with distractions and diversions keeping us from facing our pain.

For years, I was running from reality. I was running from the pain of my family being murdered and justice not being served. I have a remarkable story to tell; I truly hope this book will open your minds and hearts and spark something within you that leads you to live your life to its fullest potential. We only get one chance at life; don't waste your life fixated and focused on all the bad things that have pierced your heart. Allow your wounds to be filled with light and see how the pain can truly help you shine once you liberate yourself. Although life seems difficult at times, life is very precious and just an infinitesimal portion of eternity. What is real is your essence. The eternal light within you and within us all. Through some of my greatest suffering, I experienced some of my most profound spiritual awakenings.

My journey of self-transformation is thoroughly outlined in the following chapters and explained as practically and concretely as possible. I begin by toppling most people's perspectives on suffering. I present a new perspective flying in the face of most people's present understanding of bad events. This new outlook on suffering will serve to prime your mind for change. I begin this book on the topic of suffering because, in many ways, it epitomizes the human experience. I have found that beginning on common ground with your interlocutors is the best way to explain something, and we can all relate to pain in some way. I also begin with suffering because my own journey toward self-awareness was prompted and provoked by pain. The stories defining my journey from a life of pain to a life of both contentment and presence will serve to galvanize your own desire to better yourself. And can serve as a reference for whenever life seems to be dragging you down.

Who are you? Who is [your name]? Many people define themselves by their jobs, their friends, their family names, hometowns, and so on. Chapter two, titled "Know Thyself," teaches you to know yourself, to become cognizant of your *essence*. How to attain greater self-awareness. Many would consider the experience of losing my family as a dreadful event, but by developing the right thinking patterns, I embrace these events dearly and understand their purpose in my life.

I will then discuss the *psychology of change*, which will go over the kind of mindset I needed to adopt to see transformational progress. I will also explain some basic principles of neurology that stress the importance of living in the present moment in order to live a more stress-free life.

The book will then proceed to more actionable steps in your growth process. I will explain the daily habits I adopted to drag me out of my darkest moments. For something to be *atomic*, it is described as small in size, but powerful in effect. That, in a nutshell, is the middle portion of this book, which concerns itself primarily with intentional and unintentional habits. I explain the importance of meditation, a healthy diet, and regular exercise.

Finally, the latter part of this book deals with spirituality. Being conscious of the metaphysical serves as a bedrock, the prime motivator, and the end goal for living a happier, more content life. I will discuss the concept of *divine wisdom* and how having trust in this powerful force works as a source of infinite happiness and supreme guidance. I ask those who are irreligious or already subscribe to a particular faith to bear with me. This book does not presuppose following a particular faith, nor does it intend to exclude followers of any faith. This book is meant to be helpful to all. However, following this book in its entirety, from cover to cover, will be by far the most effective method for self-transformation.

# Part One

# 1
# Know Myself

I died for the first time when I was thirteen years old. It was a triple murder-suicide. He was an ex-NYPD officer who also happened to be my stepfather. "Frank!" my brother screamed. I rose out of bed, somehow instinctively knowing my life had been turned upside down.

The morning of June 21, 2001 was one straight out of hell.

We lived in Aurora, Colorado, a city right outside of Denver. I was in the eighth grade and known in school as the class clown for never missing an opportunity to crack a joke. I was into sports. My interest in playing football was only paralleled by my budding interest in girls.

My older brother, Mark, was similar in both respects. Mark and I always had each other growing up. We went through our parent's divorce together and we were practically abandoned in Cairo for three years and were now living in a nightmare.

Mark and I lived with my beautiful mother, Carolyn, and her then new husband, George. They had two children together: my half-sister, Gaby, and my half-baby brother, Knight. George was a retired NYPD officer and worked for the Aurora Police Department. At some point, he'd brought his job home with him and he became more aggressive and hostile toward everyone in the house.

I distinctly remember one evening in my parent's bedroom, George was changing my baby brother, Knight's, diaper. As babies usually do, Knight was kicking his legs in all directions making it look more like a wrestling match than a diaper change. With the back of his adult hand, George smacked the three-year-old with a force that could be heard from three rooms away. Within a split second, my mother charged into the room crying and yelling.

I was a few steps away from turning the corner and walking through the room door. Thud! Her head hit the wall and her whole body slammed to the ground. George was well over six feet tall and built like a linebacker. He looked at me and said, "She tried to kick me."

I stood there powerless. I was tortured by the fact that I couldn't protect my mother from the brute. Watching your own mother being abused does serious psychological damage, especially at such an impressionable age. My mother phoned the police and hysterically explained to the 911 operator the violence that had occurred. Her relief was short-lived. Two Aurora police officers, George's coworkers, towered by her while telling her that she would be jeopardizing the family if she were to press charges. They told her she would lose the kids and George would lose his job. My mother acquiesced and they successfully talked her into filing a domestic dispute instead.

Over the ensuing year, my mother and George grew further and further apart. They hardly spoke to one another and slept in different rooms. My mother made plans to move us out and to start over. George wasn't happy with my mother's plan for freedom. He even mentioned it to his coworkers at the police department. I would later learn that George explicitly told other police officers about his plan to take my mother's life. On that Thursday morning, June 21, 2001, he successfully carried out his plan.

While my brother was getting ready to leave for work, he glanced at the computer screen: "Life is a bitch, and then you die." Realizing what he had read was a suicide note, he stormed into my mother's room. I quickly did the same. I had not yet noticed the blood splattered on the room walls like an unfinished paint job. I went to wake my mother. Her blanket covered her face to her eyebrows. I shook her shoulder, but she didn't respond. I pulled the blanket down and there lay my mother's cold, stiff body with three bullets lodged in her head.

Lying right beside her was four-year-old Knight. My eyes were instantly drawn to a bright red crater right through the very cheek I once kissed and squeezed countless times before. Three bullets in his head as well. At this point, it finally registered in my mind that my mother and brother were taken by the ultimate reality of life: death. My heart sank and my hearing had become dulled as if I were underwater. I wanted to run to my sister's room but felt as though my feet were glued to the floor. My sister suffered the same gruesome fate. George was lying on the ground in a pool of his blood with a self-inflicted gunshot wound through the mouth. The pistol from hell lay right beside him.

I would not wish this nightmare on my worst enemy. My father flew from New York City to live with me. He taught himself how to drive an eighteen-wheeler so he could stay and work in Colorado. He gave me all the solace he could offer, and I am very grateful for what he did. However, I was mostly left to deal with my trauma alone. As a truck driver, my father spent days on the road away from home. My brother, dealing with this trauma as well, moved out to live with his girlfriend at the time. I felt isolated from everyone else.

The trauma was impossible for my thirteen-year-old self to handle. Everyone at school knew what happened to my family. I did my best to put on a stoic mask in front of my peers. At home, though, as soon as I removed my book bag, I would break down and weep. I was no longer the same. Once known as the class clown, I don't think I ever cracked a joke again.

To deal with the trauma, I began smoking and skipping school. At a young age, I learned to mask my pain with simple pleasures. I learned how to escape my reality with the aid of drugs and alcohol. I created detrimental habits and addictions that spiraled out of my control in the coming years. My attempt to escape from reality was the greatest tragedy of my life. I lost my true self amid the altered psychological states offered by drugs and alcohol.

After being involved in a car crash so bad they had to cut me out of the wreck, followed by a spine surgery that went awry, I found I was unable to walk. I wound up lying in a tiny studio apartment in New York City, in immense physical pain and barely able to move a limb. The only consequential act I was able to do was to ponder my past. This introspection spurred me into a depressive episode that amplified the physical pain with psychological suffering.

At that moment I went numb. Everything bottled up deep inside silently erupted. I suddenly came face-to-face with my trauma, the murder of my family, betrayal, and hopelessness. This was my awakening. My renaissance.

In the following months I set out on a plan, a course of action. I worked on mastering myself. I disciplined my body and mind. It was no easy feat. It was easier to stay in my comfort zone and continue living on autopilot. It would have been easy to allow my whims and desires to drag me down. But I onerously, consciously, and deliberately pulled myself up despite all the things working against my goal.

Today, I am a real estate investor and a personal trainer. I went from the lowest point of my life to a state of

13

contentment and happiness. During my journey of self-transformation, I failed many times, and it was those moments of failure that taught me the most. I also had many small successes that eventually made me into the person I am today. I write my story for many reasons but mainly because I sincerely believe you can take the lessons I've learned and apply them to your life. Over the past several years I have strenuously dragged myself from the deepest pits of despair to a healthy level of happiness using the following principles, which I sum up to help others battling their own demons. Whether your story resembles mine or not, committing yourself to this book will transform you into the person you ought to be.

# 2
# To Live Is to Suffer

*"The cure for pain is in the pain."*
—Rumi

Sometimes life sucks—really bad. The reality of life is that everybody experiences hardship. Some experience much, much more than others. Suffering, simply put, is pain caused by our external environment. What makes matters worse is we have little to no control over many of these circumstances. We are, nonetheless, faced with two options: We continue to consider ourselves as victims of our misfortune or we embrace the cards we are dealt and try our best to win the game. You can either lament over your circumstances or welcome your burdens with open arms, acknowledge your own shortcomings, and move on. You cannot, however, do both.

Stop resisting your reality. The Buddhists define suffering as pain combined with resistance to that pain. When we refuse to accept what has happened, we allow the suffering to linger for days, weeks, years, or even lifetimes. To resist is to do anything other than accept. Trying to escape problems is actively resisting them. Continually thinking about your problems in regret or with a feeling of guilt such as, "I should have ...," or, "I could have ..." is also resistance. This multiplies the pain, causing you to suffer not only from the calamity itself but from your own thoughts.

I have learned that in order to accept, you must cease to resist.

Oftentimes, in our attempt to avoid facing our problems, we look to simple pleasures as a means of escape. We confuse the pleasures offered by drugs, alcohol, sex, or even oversleeping with sources of happiness. I was guilty of this confusion for a long time. After seeing with my own eyes the murder of my mother, brother, and sister, I did not know how to make sense of what happened. I did not know how to cope with that trauma as a thirteen-year-old. What that actually means is I didn't know how to acknowledge the reality of their deaths and move on. Instead, I did everything I could to try to *forget* the trauma. I tried as hard as I could to run away from the facts.

At a young age, marijuana was my escape from reality. Fast forward several years and regular visits to strip clubs complemented by cocaine became what I shamefully called my lifestyle.

Accepting pain *is* painful. However, it is a necessary step in avoiding greater pain that comes with avoiding acceptance altogether. We can't change things until we recognize them as they are.

There's a story of Eastern origin that illustrates the ideas of fate and acceptance very well. There once lived a king who, wherever he went, always brought his most trusted adviser along. This king loved to hunt. For whenever his kingdom was at peace, he would plan weekend-long hunting trips for him and his adviser. The two were very different people. The adviser grew up in the poorest slums of the kingdom. He joined the military and climbed the ranks to eventually become one of the most trusted aides to the throne.

The king, on the other hand, was from a long lineage of royalty and could not think of even a remote relative who ever worked a day in their life. While hunting, the king spotted a deer. He pulled the arrow back against the bowstring and right before he released the arrow, he mistakenly moved his finger. The bow almost sliced his finger off. The king was in immense pain and his finger was gushing blood. His adviser, who was standing next to him, told the king, "Everything happens for your own good." The king, whose burning red face matched the color of his wound, believed the adviser's remark to be insensitive and ordered him to be locked away immediately.

The king carried on hunting by himself. Shortly after, members of a native tribe captured the king. They dragged him to a campfire where he soon realized he was about to be their lunch. As they were tying his arms and legs around a ten-foot-long log resembling a human shish kebab, they noticed the cut on the king's finger. They threw their arms up and said, "He's damaged; we can't offer him as a sacrifice." They proceeded to untie him and let him go.

Upon his arrival back to the kingdom, the king saw his adviser and told him what had happened to him.

"You were right," he said, with a rare display of humility. "That cut turned out to be for my own good." The humility turned out to be short-lived as his ego once again took over and he added, "But you're in a jail cell, how could that be for your own good, huh?"

"My fingers are fine; if I were with you, I would have been lunch," the adviser wisely replied.

This story is simple, but its simplicity is key to allowing us to extract the core lessons. In one word, the core of this story—and by extension, our entire lives' stories— would be the power that resides within *retrospection*. The axiom presented to us by the adviser, "*Everything that happens to us is good*," at first glance seems like an irritating moment of false optimism, but its message is later corroborated by the fact that an earlier incident thought to be unfavorable turned out to be the best thing to ever happen to the king. However, it was only understood to be good in light of the following events, when the tribesmen saw the king unworthy because of his blemish.

This is the power of retrospect: It allows us to be able to make sense of things. Retrospect gives value to events, namely positive value, such as something being "good." This perspective makes it easier to *accept* because events are no longer understood in isolation, but rather as small pieces to a greater puzzle. I hope this clarifies the link between acceptance and retrospect. The following will delve deeper into the role of retrospect and reflection, which will further clarify the importance and imperative of acceptance.

## *Amor fati*

There was once a television series writer who had written a new show that was set to be aired. The writer had been invited on a discussion panel to talk about his new show. Along with the show's writer, actor George Carlin was also invited on the panel. The writer was asked to briefly explain the plot of his new show:

"*It's about a train, and it's sort of a magic train, a train that defies all universal laws. You can buy a ticket for this train that allows you to go back to any point in your life. Any moment at all where you wanna start over. And when you get on the train, you'll notice that I'm the conductor,*" the writer said.

"*Yea, I can think of a couple of things that I would have done differently. I think anyone can think of times in their lives that they would go back and change*," replied another person on the panel.

"*No, I don't think so*," George Carlin interjected. "*If I went back and changed anything that had happened in my life, I wouldn't be me, and I like me*."

Acceptance is necessary but embracing is even better. The wisest minds throughout history understood the power of taking acceptance a step further: to *embrace* all that happens to you. To understand the dichotomy of control. So much of what happens to you is out of your control, such as unexpected events and the behaviors of other people.

We do, however, have direct control over our conscious thoughts and actions. We also have control over the effort we put into things. We have control over our attitude and our perceptions of the world. And that is where our focus lies. We must focus on our perception of the world, and not necessarily the world itself. We can control how we feel about things. We can control our expectations and our actions going forward.

To embrace our fate means to genuinely love everything that comes our way—both the good and the bad. The concept of *amor fati*, which translates to love your fate, was introduced by the Stoics and made popular by nineteenth-century philosopher Friedrich Nietzsche. Epictetus, a stoic philosopher who was enslaved for many years of his life, writes:

> *Do not seek for things to happen the way you want*
> *them to; rather, wish that what happens happen the*
> *way it happens: then you will be happy.*

To embrace your fate, and essentially your entire being as you are today, presupposes the acceptance of every second of your existence.

So which experiences should we perceive as negative and warrant a negative reaction? The answer, logically speaking, is none. No event can logically be said to be a good or bad event. According to eighteenth-century Scottish philosopher David Hume, there exists a gap in reasoning when trying to conclude whether any event should have or should not have happened. From this, we derive what's called a "fact-value distinction," which asserts that to deem any fact, event, or object as inherently bad or good is illogical.

Things don't happen *to us*. They just happen. "The universe is indifferent."

For example, in the story above, was the king's injury a good or bad thing? We cannot know for certain. In an immediate time frame, the king's injury seemed like a bad thing. Within the context of a long-term series of events, the injury turned out to save his life, and preservation of life is ostensibly a good thing. An event can only be interpreted in the context of a goal, an aim to be sought after. Shooting oneself with an arrow may be a good thing to a masochist, but then again his injury prevented him from further pain, thus not being a good thing for a masochist. So, without delving too deep into philosophical discourse, we can conclude here by saying that any event that happens to you is neither good nor bad.

Knowing that every event that happens to you is neutral in value can free you from the obligation of reacting emotionally to the things that happen to you. No experience in your past calls for a sad or regretful response when looking retrospectively. And similarly, no event in the future warrants anxiety or stress, according to logic.

When we come to realize that the value of events is what we ourselves voluntarily assign to them, we are able to emotionally detach from the things that happen to us, specifically negative emotions such as feelings of guilt, grief, sadness, anxiety, and so on. Psychiatrist Viktor E. Frankl, who lived through the horrors of the Holocaust and wrote extensively about his experiences in the Nazi concentration camps, stated:

> *Between stimulus and response there is a space. In that space is our power to choose our response. In our response lies our growth and our freedom.*

We are not compelled to give a particular response to things or even any response at all. The *space* mentioned here is akin to Hume's gap in reasoning mentioned above, in the sense that there is a separation between the physical, external world and our internal judgment. Knowing that it is us who connects the external with the internal, the physical with the psychological, that we give the value to the events in our lives allows us to be free from the chains of emotion, reflect objectively, learn from our past, and prepare for the future.

Now that you understand that no event is necessarily good or bad, how can you use that to learn to embrace your fate? First, we must understand that the person you are today is a function of all your life events combined. It can be mapped out like this:

*Current you = (all past events) + (genetic predisposition)*

This means that all that has happened to you, whether you perceive those experiences to be good or bad, are a part of what makes you *uniquely* you. It follows then that to loathe a singular event in your life may amount to self-loathing. If you are unhappy with even the smallest fraction of your life then you open the door for being unhappy about your current self.

To be clear, I am not arguing that one should smooth over their life with fictitious optimism. Rather, simply be content with your past and all that you have gone through. To not ruminate over any second of your past but to acknowledge it as a constant fact of your existence.

## Gratitude

Gratitude is the atomic ingredient in transforming the things we accept into the things we embrace. Gratitude is a *deep* appreciation for what one receives. Gratitude is an emotion, a response to a *gift*. It's a psychological state that occurs when one is the beneficiary of a selfless act that was unexpected, undeserved, and unearned. Gratitude is not transactional in a way a merchant thanks their patrons, rather it is associated with receiving something that was never owed in the first place.

In March 2017, I woke up in a hospital bed in Manhattan, New York, not able to move a muscle from the waist down. I was undergoing spine surgery to treat injuries I sustained from a car accident. I was in immense physical and psychological pain. The simple task of turning my 150-pound body to either side was dreadfully painful. Being utterly dependent on the nurses for the most menial tasks of life such as using the bathroom was shamefully depressing. Once again, I thought I hit rock bottom. I was suffering from both the bodily pain and the "why me" moans. I lamented over my life once again, drawing connections between the death of my family and my virtual paralysis, to conclude that life is cruel and I am its hopeless victim. I looked to my left and on the hospital bed on the opposite side of the room, I saw a young man staring straight at me.

"Hey, I'm Gabe," he said, sporting a contagious smile.

"Frank, nice to meet you," I replied. He asked why I was there, and I explained. I asked him the same question. The look in his eyes signaled a sense of relief as if he were waiting for someone to ask him that question, or any question at all.

"Lung cancer. I've been battling it for almost a year now. The doctors finally told me I have two weeks to live," he said calmly.

"How did your family take the news?" I asked.

"I haven't spoken to them in months," Gabe replied. My heart sunk and I instantly felt a rush of secondhand discomfort. I knew exactly how it felt to be alone. To be all by yourself when your world feels like it's crashing down, and I felt it again just listening to this young man's story.

Gabe taught me a greater lesson: to be grateful for not only my blessings but also to appreciate the misfortune that I am lucky enough to call my own. Television broadcaster Robin Roberts said:

*I bet if we all threw our problems in a huge pile and saw everyone else's, we'd rush to grab ours back.*

Being grateful for all the good in our life is obvious. But to be grateful for having that which causes us pain seems a bit unnatural. Things could be worse, and that's not merely a platitude; it's a fact. The life you are living is a dream for many others.

I should take a step back and say that I am not advocating a form of shallow comparison in which one looks at others worse off than themselves to feel good. That is not gratitude. Gratitude is to remind yourself constantly that you are in a great position in life. You are blessed, and oftentimes it may take a glance at others to remind you of how well you are doing.

For you to indulge in the feeling of gratitude, you must first *acknowledge* the good in your life that you are privileged to enjoy. And secondly, *recognize* that this good stems from somewhere outside yourself. To transcend the self and give credit for the good of your own life to God, or the universe, or probability, or whatever you think is the reason for your blessings. This is most important because we cannot feel gratitude while thinking only of ourselves and our own accomplishments. We must turn our back to the mirror, leave our ego at the door, and appreciate that which is *not* one's own self.

So far, we have talked about the importance of acceptance as a necessary first step toward finding inner peace. We then took it a step further and discussed the power of loving all the events of your life. Followed by how the power of gratitude gives reinforces the concept of *amor fati*. The following clarifies these abstractions by explaining how to effectively reflect on your suffering and squeeze *meaning* out of the tumult of life.

# 3
# Know Thyself

*"Life can only be understood backwards;*
*but it must be lived forwards."*
—Søren Kierkegaard

A jigsaw puzzle is a picture printed on a piece of cardboard, which is then cut into many different pieces of weird shapes. When separated from the rest of the pieces, a single piece makes absolutely no sense. When all the separated pieces are spread out on the floor, it also makes no sense. It is only when each piece is ordered and placed in the right position relative to the other pieces does each piece possess *meaning*.

Our lives are analogous to a puzzle: Each individual event is a constituent piece of a greater picture. If we look at each event in isolation, it makes no sense, or even worse, we take that event for face value. It is only when we consciously piece the events together, that we can extract a greater picture. For a puzzle to be completed, someone has to sit on the floor for hours, onerously but intentionally making sense of what seems to be an incoherent pile of pieces. The same is true for your life as well. This brings me to reflection.

I want to come back to life's biggest mystery, the subject of suffering, to illustrate the utility of reflection in making sense of suffering. Like the puzzle, if we make a habit of looking at the events of our lives or pieces in isolation, then we inevitably fall into the perilous act of understanding, or misunderstanding that is, suffering as only that and nothing more. But if we take even the ugliest moments of our lives, and plug them into the right places, we can't help but focus on the greater picture. Even the *Mona Lisa* can be cut up and pieced apart.

How beautiful it is to suffer then. But why me? These were my thoughts exactly. I was waking up in a New York City studio apartment the size of some people's walk-in closet. Those days are marked as the days I jerked my feet every time I heard a squeak, unsure whether it was a starving mouse in my apartment or the "7" train coming to a halt. I was thirty years old and learning how to walk. I was struggling to use the bathroom. A rerun of my regretful past played in my head only interrupted by the piercing pain of the mattress springs I was lying on. I cried regularly almost to the point of blindness. After I drained myself of all my tears there was nothing left for me to do. I was lying in numbness, not too far from total death. I soaked in the suffering, passively, without putting up a fight. Like a dead fish in a tsunami. It was then that I acknowledged the fact that at my lowest point no one is coming to save me.

This was my epiphany. This was when I decided to take control of my life. This is where I thought to myself:

*"I can either be a victim or a victor of my reality, but I cannot be both."*

And I promised myself I will live the rest of my life by those words. I realized that while it is true that some events in my life are out of my control, the murder of my mother and two siblings when I was thirteen years old was not my fault, and as we spoke about earlier, it was important for me to accept that. What was my fault, however, was how I dealt with it.

Self-reflection is to take a deep look inward. It is to sincerely analyze ourselves to learn and grow. Self-reflection is more than just probing your past. It means to evaluate your behaviors, thoughts, attitudes, motivations, and desires, and to ask ourselves the *why* behind each one of these.

Through the process of self-reflection, we identify what we do well and commend ourselves on it. But more importantly, we realize our weaknesses and address them. Through reflection, we come face-to-face with our weaknesses. No one likes to ponder on their own faults and failures. Our ego finds it discomforting. But within temporary discomfort often lies growth.

In essence, self-reflection is a form of active learning. We learn about the most important topic to us, ourselves, through studying our past. The American philosopher and education reformer John Dewey said:

*We do not learn from experience ... we learn from reflecting on experience.*

Simply living through the events of our lives is not enough. We must intentionally ponder on our experiences and make sense of them. And we must do this routinely. This means you must have a sincere conversation with yourself. In mathematical terms, pain + reflection = progress.

In my case, self-reflection meant taking responsibility for who I had become. When I was in that studio apartment, my spine injury made me unable to move. I didn't have a television set so the only thing I could do was think. However, thinking does not necessarily result in reflection. I started off with a regretful kind of thinking. A very unhealthy kind that is probably best characterized as a depressive episode. I was missing the element of curiosity in order for my thinking to be self-reflection.

I had to detach any emotion from my thinking, for my reflection on the past to be useful. I realized that the reason why I had never fruitfully reflected before was that I always looked at the past in an emotional light. Like a small domino leading up to bigger ones, everything in one's life is connected, and before my epiphany, I tied everything in my life to the murder of my family.

Feelings of anger, guilt, hate, mourning and a sense of vulnerability were all bottled up inside of me. These feelings permeated every thought I had ever conceived. I, until that day of reflection, couldn't escape those feelings.

Reflection brought me face-to-face with what I had been avoiding my whole life. Through reflection, I was able to track down the core motivations for all my decisions, attitudes, and behaviors, much like how a detective tracks down a culprit.

The underpinnings for my behavior stemmed from that undealt with trauma. From my reflection, I realized it took me almost two decades to accept the murder of my family. Acceptance allowed me to take responsibility for my actions. And only through taking responsibility was I able to change myself. All of this was a result of reflection. I began scheduling time to reflect by journaling my thoughts in a notebook every day. This helped me understand my thoughts better, and in turn, better understand myself.

These three elements, (1) understanding myself through reflection, (2) accepting my past, and (3) changing myself, operate in somewhat of a feedback mechanism. The more you practice reflection, the more you will evaluate and understand yourself. A better understanding of who you are and who you want to be will drive you to move toward an improved version of yourself. And finally, the improved version of yourself is more inclined to reflect and refine themselves.

So, although I have introduced acceptance before reflection, I want you to think of reflection as a broad concept that encompasses acceptance within it. Therefore, in a sense, reflection comes in two forms: *initial reflection* into who you are and *reflection with the intention to change yourself.* Acceptance comes somewhere in between these two. Embracing your fate follows the second form of reflection because it is a result of that reflection. Loving your fate is inevitably brought about when you ascribe meaning to your life events.

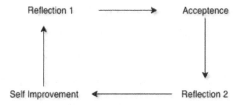

The analogy of the jigsaw puzzle is directly related to loving your fate, and by extension, also related to acceptance. The role of reflection here is to attribute meaning to each part of your life. Each event, whether you perceive that event to be good or bad, has meaning in the grand scheme of things, just as each piece of a puzzle serves a purpose.

Reflection enables you to mend order out of chaos. Without reflection, life is just a loose collection of events, with no clear and concise purpose. But you are greater than that. Life is a coherent story. Each event has a purpose. There are no losses in life when everything is a lesson. And the beauty of a lesson is, if it's retained, it travels with you wherever you go.

Everything you do is at least in part motivated by some lesson you learned earlier in life. So, the unique way in which you operate today is related, whether directly or indirectly, to a lesson you learned before. Therefore, any experience in your life, as long as you extract some lesson from it, is to be embraced.

There are reasons to appreciate the bad in your life. The suffering I endured gave my life direction. It pushed me to question myself. The accumulated pain that built up and fermented within me was unleashed in that studio apartment that morning. It put me in the position to reflect. Before I reflected, I understood the death of my family as just murder, and only that. But that is not all it was. Like a single piece of a jigsaw puzzle, my family's death was an event that represents one constituent piece of a bigger picture.

It was that reflection that set me on the course to change and inevitably write this book. The pain brought about when I was thirteen and the pain in that studio apartment, and all the hardship in between, are an indispensable part of my story. The story you are reading right now and hopefully the story that, in doing your part, will change your life as well.

The pain in my life also moved me toward being more compassionate toward others. If we were never afflicted with pain, how would we know how to feel when others are going through hard times? The extent of our compassion would be limited to imagination. We understand most of those who have been in similar positions as ourselves. Could you imagine a life without pain?

There are countless reasons why we should appreciate the suffering we go through, and it is through this reasoning we can put life in perspective to appreciate what we have and what we have been through, both the good and the bad. This is reflection.

## Reflection for self-awareness

*"Your visions will become clear only when you can look into your own heart. Who looks outside, dreams; who looks inside, awakes."*
—Carl G. Jung

The crown jewel of reflection is attaining self-awareness. Self-awareness is the ability to see yourself objectively. To understand who you are and who you are not. The act of reflection aids in the discovery of our true selves, which for many, may take a whole lifetime before they get to know who they really are.

American actor and comedian Jim Carrey once said:

*Depression is your avatar telling you it's tired of being the character you are trying to play.*

Many found this statement to suggest a dualistic nature of the self: you, and the character you are trying to play. But who really was Jim Carrey and which part of himself was he tired of being?

Jim Carrey was born on January 17, 1962, in Ontario, Canada. His father, Percy, was a talented musician and comedian who, despite his love for music and comedy, decided to suppress his artistic side in favor of a more financially stable career as an accountant. Jim Carrey seemed to inherit his father's aptitude for comedy but not his father's aversion to risk which was clear when Carrey pursued a career in stand-up comedy. After a rough start and being booed off stage several times, Jim gradually found success in Canada's comedy sphere when was discovered by Rodney Dangerfield and was brought to Las Vegas as the opening act. Carrey quickly gained popularity in the US and landed a role on the sketch comedy show *In Living Color*. He later went on to make a series of blockbuster hits, including *Dumb and Dumber*, *Ace Ventura*, *The Mask*, and *Man on the Moon*—catapulting him to superstardom.

It had been made public that Carrey was diagnosed with major depressive disorder. He was taking Prozac, a medication to treat the illness, which in his words "feels like a low level of despair that you're in. You're not getting any answers but you're living okay and smiling at the office … but it's a low level of despair." He began his search into who he truly was. He began to reflect.

Carrey decided to stop taking Prozac and instead turned toward spirituality and art as a refuge. He stopped consuming any kinds of drugs, alcohol, and coffee. His problems with depression subsided and he does not experience it regularly anymore. He said, "I had [depression] for years, but now, when the rain comes, it rains, but it doesn't stay. It doesn't stay long enough to immerse me and drown me anymore."

Jim Carrey discovered himself in 1999, five years after the death of his father, on the set of filming the comedy-drama *Man on the Moon*. This marked the start of his journey of discovering himself. He was playing the role of Andy Kaufman, a comedian whom Carrey looked up to growing up. He completely immersed himself in the role. Almost becoming Kaufman and leaving behind his old self.

By stepping into the point of view of someone else, he objectively took a look at who Jim Carrey was. He questioned all assumptions. It was a completely new perspective for Carrey. In 2017 a Netflix documentary sought to publish the behind-the-scenes footage from *Man on the Moon* and gather insight on Carrey's moments of transformation. In the documentary, Carrey is interviewed and emerges sporting a big beard and a leather jacket reminiscent of a modern-day philosopher.

"When did this transition take place?" the interviewer asked.

"Somewhere in the middle of absolute confusion, absolute disappointment … the fruition of all of my dreams standing there with everything anybody else had ever dreamed about having and being unhappy."

Being able to play Kaufman showed him what it was like to momentarily stop being him. He expresses his awakening beautifully by saying, "Who's Jim Carrey? Oh yeah, he doesn't exist. There's just a relative manifestation of consciousness appearing, and then somebody gave him a bunch of ideas; a name, a religion, and a nationality, and he clustered those together into something that is supposed to be a personality."

For Carrey, it was the experience of playing the part of his former role model that brought him to a spiritual crisis. To question and seek answers. He found himself and it wasn't the same person he was before. Carrey discovered his spiritual self and realized he did not need medication for him to be *normal*. As an actor, Carrey was privileged, in a sense, in that it was his job to detach his conscious mind from himself.

Perhaps that is why we always hear of an actor going through mental illness. Jim Carrey was able to gain self-awareness by stepping out of himself and observing his programs. Detaching his conscious mind from his ego. Eckhart Tolle explains:

> *When you no longer believe everything you think, you step out of thought and see clearly that the thinker is not who you are.*

While you may not be an actor, you are able to do the same thing through introspection and meditation. It is your turn to observe yourself. Take a journal and break down who you are. Ask yourself a series of questions as if you are taking yourself on a date. Start with simple questions such as what do I do well? What are my weaknesses? When do I feel my happiest? What am I doing when I feel like I am at my lowest? Slowly go deeper. Read your answers out loud so you can be more conscious of them. Remember, the goal here is to find out the whys behind everything you do. Gaining self-awareness through meditation will be explained in the later chapters on meditation.

# Part Two

# 4

# Psychology of Change

*"For as he thinks in his heart, so is he."*
—Proverbs 23:7

A Zen master was walking in an open field one morning when he saw a horse galloping toward him at full speed. Mounted on the horse was a young man who was looking in the direction of where the horse was going. The horseman and his horse came within a few inches of the Zen master. The Zen master asked the horseman, "Where are you going?" The horse sprinted away from the Zen master without leaving a moment for the horseman to answer. He yelled from a distance, "I don't know! Ask the horse."

The subconscious mind controls much of what we do. Some estimate that the subconscious dictates 95 percent of the average person's day. So, what exactly is the subconscious? In contrast to the conscious mind, which is rational and deliberate, the subconscious mind is irrational and involuntary. So, we should be concerned when an irrational system attempts to hijack 95 percent of our life.

In the story above, the horse symbolizes the subconscious, and the rider is the conscious. The horse ultimately dictated the direction the two were going, and not the rider. Similarly, it is the subconscious part of our mind that is in control. The horse overpowered the rider, much like how the subconscious overpowers the conscious. If the rider does not take control of the horse, his destination will be left completely to the whim of the horse; likewise, if you do not intentionally and meticulously master your subconscious, it will live your life for you.

The subconscious mind functions like a database that stores every thought, perception, and experience you ever had. It pieces these bits of information together to form a belief system about itself. The belief system that your subconscious creates dictates your future thoughts, beliefs, and eventually actions. The following explains part of the subconscious's function as a decision maker.

Psychologists have divided the cognition process of the human brain into two: a slow, deliberate form of thinking and a fast, instinctive kind. Psychologist and Nobel Prize winner Daniel Kahneman has dedicated his life to research the process of decision-making. He was inspired to research rational thinking when he came across a fundamental assumption in economic theory: the assumption that humans are rational actors. Kahneman, being a psychologist by profession, saw this as contradictory to his own field of practice.

Kahneman set out on the mission to explore why we as humans are so bad at making rational decisions. Why does our mind play tricks on us when we are thinking? Those who are familiar with his work will understand the many reasons that explain our faulty thinking.

Slow thinking is a calculated, intentional kind of thinking that is best characterized as a *conscious* state of mind. What is the answer to 200 minus 112? When trying to answer this question, you are undergoing a calculative kind of decision-making process using the conscious mind. You use this mode of thinking when you are learning something new or doing something you don't usually do. The first time you drove a car you were learning how to shift gears and flick the turn signal up and down by using your slow and deliberate mechanism of thinking. For the purposes of this book, we will call this mode of thinking *conscious thinking*.

In contrast, fast thinking is reactive and almost instinctual. Emotional responses to stimuli fall into this category. Fast thinking is the result of the accumulation of things you have done many times before until they have become entrenched in your mind as autonomic thoughts and habits.

What is 2 plus 2? You probably didn't have to count on your fingers or use a pen and paper to calculate the answer. Instead, you knew it from memory. That is your subconscious mind tackling that question. After spending some time driving, flicking the turn signal up for right and down for left needs not any deliberation either. And you've probably noticed how when you're driving on an open road, you can have full conversations with your passengers or on the phone? That is because you have driven so many times before it becomes automatic. It is your fast, subliminal state of mind that is operating the vehicle. You don't have to think about it. We will call this mode of thinking subconscious thinking.

The main difference between the two is how deliberate you are when completing a task. Let us pretend your mind is a computer. When you turn on your computer, enter your password, double-click an Internet browser, and type something on a keyboard, these actions are all intentional. You are aware of these actions because you had to manually perform them. Between all these physical actions, are millions of computational steps that occur in the background that the user is never aware of. The user has no idea about the built-in software that was *programmed* into the computer's operating chip and installed by the software engineer, then later altered by some malware accidentally downloaded from surfing the Web. This is analogous to how your brain operates. The manual inputs by the user such as entering a password and launching applications can represent your conscious mind. The programming built into the motherboard is equivalent to your subconscious. And in a computer, the programming is ultimately in control. The applications and functions can only be used if the programming allows for it. The user is subject to the nature of the software. This is also true of the mind. The subconscious is ultimately in control. Your conscious thoughts are largely the product of your subconscious. And in the context of self-transformation, changing yourself means reprogramming your subconscious.

When it comes to effort, your mind treats it as a commodity and uses effort conservatively. And since we now know that conscious thinking is deliberate and more effortful, our mind by default skews toward using our subconscious process of thinking. This is because of our mind's limited capacity of *working memory*. Consider the number 4632. Now add 3 to every digit of that number. The result would be 7965. If repeated, it would be 0298. Now I want you to look away and repeat this step of adding 3 to each number. The ability to carry out several mental functions simultaneously, such as adding 3 to four different numbers, is the function of working memory. Working memory is exclusively within the capacity of our conscious mental process. To do this task continually requires focus and effort, and after a while, we begin to lose focus. This is likely because evolutionarily, our ancestors couldn't be so tunnel-visioned on a task for so long without thinking of predators or some other survival thought. I explain this to illustrate how naturally averse we are to being conscious.

Kahneman's research teaches us that our thinking is riddled with biases, heuristics, and emotions. Ever heard the phrase "emotions cloud your judgment"? This is because of the sheer dominance of our visceral thoughts, that is, the subconscious. It is our biases and irrational thoughts that direct our rational thoughts. As philosopher David Hume once said, "Reason is the slave of passions," similarly, the conscious is a slave of the subconscious. In sum, if you only take one thing from this chapter it should be this: your subconscious is ultimately in control.

To change yourself through reflection, you need to think clearly. You need to be aware of your biases. Recognize when you're not thinking rationally and when your irrational mind is taking over. Now apply the information above to the process of reflection. Detach emotion from logic, and reflect.

## *My wrestle with the subconscious*

It took me four hours to walk a distance that would take most people fifteen minutes. In 2017, a car accident left me barely able to walk. Despite this, with my walker in hand and my back hunched like an old person, I forced myself to journey a two-mile distance from my father's apartment to the Queens piers that overlooked the Manhattan skyline. Every step of the way was mechanical. The disks of my spine felt glued together as any bending movement would bring extreme pain. It also happened to be during an arctic blast that winter, which to my luck hasn't happened in NY for a long time. But still, I pushed. I felt every second of the four-hour journey. My borderline frost-bitten hands continued to hold my metal walker with the wind blowing right in my face. And still, I pushed.

My dreadful walk symbolized the end of my old self. That if I wanted to reach my goals, I would have to push through the pain. Getting rid of bad habits is hard, and developing new ones is no easy feat either. But still, I had to push through the pain.

The pain I felt during my walk brought me to the present moment because the only way I was able to keep going, to put one foot in front of the other, was by staying in the present. My subconscious wanted to stop. My body was telling me to go back to the warm comfort indoors. But to reach my destination, I had to drag myself intentionally, forcefully, and painfully. Every step was a battle, and in the end, I was victorious.

Through reflection, I noticed I had toxic thinking patterns. Ever since the death of my mother I was pretty much raising myself. I didn't have any adult guidance. The people I was hanging around with were drug dealers from the neighborhood. The more I was around them, the more I became just like them. Soon enough, I too started selling cocaine and marijuana. I began listening to "gangster rap" music. The clothes I wore increased by two sizes and I sported my jeans below my waist. In short, I conformed to my immediate surroundings.

I adopted mannerisms, language, and ways of thinking from the people I was around. The subconscious mind is always on. It is always learning, even when you don't think it is.

They say a child is like a sponge because they learn from everything around them; this is also true of the subconscious. The subconscious mind functions like a huge memory bank. It stores every thought and every experience you ever had, like a database, then tries to make sense of it. From this database, your subconscious attempts to construct a master program. It tries to decide who you are. It essentially attempts to mold your character based on your experiences. We will call this your *master programming.* Your subconscious interprets every thought and event in a way that conforms to your existing self-concept, which is your subconscious's understanding of who you are. The good news is through discipline and commitment, you can rewrite your master programs.

## *The three parts of thought*

When I set out on the effort to better myself, I quickly noticed that the forces that were working against me most were within myself. I was my greatest enemy. But how could this be? If I have one brain, and I am operating from my brain in a conscious effort to change myself for the better, what is it that can possibly work against me?

I discovered that different portions of the brain are responsible for different kinds of cognitive behavior. Depending on which part of my brain is active at the time, my decision-making and overall behavior will be different. Intentionality and deliberateness, both needed for greater consciousness, are hindered when our cognitive activity is not in the frontal lobe.

1.  The reptilian brain (automatic)
2.  The limbic (automatic)
3.  The neocortex (deliberate)

The reptilian brain is the oldest of the three, evolutionarily speaking, and is responsible for regulating *automatic* mechanisms such as breathing and heartbeat. It is notoriously attributed to the "four Fs": feeding, fighting, fleeing, and … [reproduction].

The limbic brain developed after the reptilian, and it is the seat of *emotion*. The limbic brain attributes value judgments to memories, which deem whether something is good or bad. There are three main structures of the limbic brain: the hippocampus, the amygdala, and the hypothalamus.

The reptilian and limbic brains both function in a reactive way and are instinctual in nature. They closely resemble the System 1 thinking by Daniel Kahneman that we discussed earlier, which is the fast kind of thinking responsible for many cognitive errors and biases.

Finally, the neocortex is the most complex partition of the brain and is where conscious thought resides. This part matches System 2 thinking that is slow and deliberate. It is responsible for higher states of thought, such as critical thinking and compassion. A developed neocortex is what sets humans apart from other animals because it makes it possible for compassion, imagination, creativity, language, and all other elements of intelligent life. We want to spend more of our lives operating from the neocortex, and less from the limbic and reptilian brain. We want to cultivate the neocortex and its ability for complex thought, and at the same time use the neocortex to control the impulses from primitive portions of the brain.

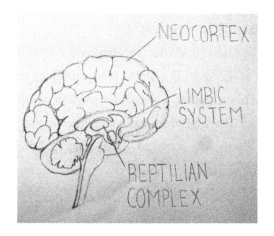

## Your childhood programs

In his book *Rich Dad Poor Dad*, Robert Kiyosaki
writes about two fathers; one is a high school dropout, and the
other is well educated with multiple advanced degrees.
Kiyosaki writes about growing up going to school with many
children of wealthy families, while he came from a family of
modest earnings. His father was the father with multiple
degrees, but throughout the book, he called him the "poor
dad." His friend's father was the "rich dad"; however, the
highest education the rich dad received was at the high school
level. In his book, Kiyosaki writes about why he thinks the
rich stay rich, and the poor stay poor. Why are children of
wealthy parents more likely to become wealthy themselves,
while the children of poor parents are more likely to stay
poor?

Kiyosaki concludes that it is the financial habits that
dictate whether one will be wealthy or not, and these habits
are passed down from parents to children subconsciously. He
says a dumb person may end up being successful, while an
intelligent person may end up broke, simply because of the
financial habits they have. These habits are usually passed
down unintentionally, by just watching what our parents do.
When entertaining the thought of buying something out of the
boundaries of their budgets, Kiyosaki explains the difference
between the rich father and the poor father this way:

*One dad had a habit of saying, 'I can't afford it.' The other dad forbade those words to be used. He insisted I ask, "How can I afford it?" One is a statement, and the other is a question. One lets you off the hook, and the other forces you to think.*

While Kiyosaki writes about financial literacy, his work illustrates how powerful our subconscious programming is in all fields of life, highlighting the urgency to focus on ourselves. Bad habits can offset the benefits of education, and good habits can multiply it.

Before I go in-depth about the rituals that transformed me, it would be best understood if you were to know the psychological underpinnings of how the mind is hardwired. You now know how the subconscious works, and that it is ultimately in control, every thought you have is ultimately facilitated by an intuitive impulse. Let's investigate how you developed your programs.

The Jesuits have a saying:

*Give us a child till he's seven and we'll have him for life.*

This saying gives us a good idea about how we developed into who we are today. The inputs of our early childhood make up the bulk of our personalities. Sociologists studying the development of children conclude that above all the other factors, a child's family is by far the most impactful agent of socialization. So I want you to be aware of all the programs that you may have adopted from your family. The way you act is directly impacted by the way your parents, siblings, and all those whom you were around acted during your childhood. Through reflection, we need to identify and isolate these common behaviors. Now that you are aware of the programs you have involuntarily downloaded into your subconscious, you have to intentionally decide whether to keep these behaviors or not. A Harvard study found that in families where one parent is depressed, about 40 percent of youths develop depression by age twenty, and 60 percent do so by age twenty-five. That's twice the likelihood compared to children in a household without a depressed parent. Even when considering the possibility that many cases of depression may have been genetically passed down, the numbers are still alarming. This highlights the impact on our mentality those around us have. You need to be selective with what you allow your subconscious to be exposed to, and even though your childhood may have long been in the past, through reflection we may go back in time and identify the unwanted behaviors. Simply becoming aware that you have the behavior is half the job already. The other half is eliminating that behavior from your subconscious by using the *rituals of change.*

Today, it may not be your family that makes up the bulk of your input but make no mistake your subconscious is still very amenable. Take a moment to reflect on your environment. Reflect on the people around you. Meditate on the shows you watch, the music you listen to, and probably most relevant to the twenty-first century, the content you see on social media. We used to say you are the average of the five people you hang out with the most; nowadays we should say you are the average of the social media pages you interact with the most.

## How powerful is the subconscious?

*Our behaviors, thoughts, and experiences are a manifestation of the subconscious, and the subconscious is a composite of our past behaviors, thoughts, and experiences.* You might have to read that again. In other words, the relationship between the subconscious and fate is somewhat cyclical in nature. One feeds into the other and vice versa. This linkage means that if we change one, we indirectly change the other. Psychologist Carl Jung said:

> *Until you make the unconscious conscious,*
> *it will direct your life and you will call it fate.*

This is where we take responsibility for ourselves entirely. You have now been made aware of the fact that you have the power to change yourself. This is where you stop blaming your upbringing. Your genetics. Your childhood trauma. And everything else you thought you had no control over. I am fully aware of the impact that all of these factors can have on the human mindset. But after reading this, you are now aware that you can have an even greater impact on your mind that can offset that damage done by negative experiences, and multiply your potential. The torch is in your hands now. Carl Jung also said:

*I am not what happened to me, I am what I choose to become.*

By turning away from change, you have chosen a path of weakness, lethargy, and pity. The onus is now more than ever on you.

When we leave our subconscious to its own devices, we allow it to reinforce our dispositional programming. For emphasis, I want to repeat the fact that your subconscious mind is ALWAYS WORKING. It is always listening and expanding its memory bank. It's virtually limitless in capacity. As the days pass, the subconscious continues to expand, thus further consolidating the power of the dispositional programming it has devised.

Therefore we are always susceptible to internalizing the negativity in our environment. We absorb the thoughts of those around us and our subconscious makes sense of it in some way. Actions committed by us and others are mentally noted. Every statement said by us about ourselves is recorded and interpreted by our subconscious mind. And I repeat once again: Your subconscious mind is ALWAYS WORKING. The people you are around, whether family, friends, coworkers, or strangers, are shaping who you are.

Motivational speaker David Brown once said that you are the average of the five people you spend the most time with. This is because of your subconscious's nature of perceptual learning and its composite of mirror neurons. Because of the mirror neuron system, when we are around happy people, we become happy. When we are around stressed people, we too become stressed. When we surround ourselves with positivity, we are more likely to reflect a positive lifestyle. You should guard against who you let around you, and what environment you allow yourself to be in because all of it contributes to who you *become*.

The television programming you watch is exactly that: *programming*. You are by way of eyes and ears, indirectly shaping yourself. Studies show that children who watch more than two hours of television a day exhibit more aggressive behavior and fewer communication skills than children who watch less. The lyrics in the rap music I was listening to permeated my subconscious with thoughts of the criminal lifestyle. Sex, drugs, and money were idolized in that music genre. It was no surprise, then, that that was the kind of lifestyle I was attracted to and identified with.

I wasn't aware then of what I know now so I let myself be subjected to the whims of music, the people around me, and my overall environment. I mirrored the nature of all of those and it made me who I was. However, "being unaware" was never an adequate excuse. I always knew that the content in the music was objectively bad—I mean, have you ever listened to American rap and hip-hop music? I always knew that the people around me were not the best people to be around. I knew all of those things, so how come I didn't do anything about it? Because I underestimated their effect. I told myself that I was in control of myself. I told myself that the music I listened to and the environment I was in would not affect my life as long as I didn't let it. "It doesn't really matter," I said. Boy, was I wrong.

News flash: Everything matters! All the little things matter. Over time, the little things accumulate and become big things. In my case, they made me who I was.

Given the nature of the subconscious, it lacks any critical thinking or scrutinization of the information that slips into it, meaning it pretty much swallows everything wholesale. Even the thoughts you jokingly say to yourself are contributing to your master program. Sociologist Charles

Cooley posited his theory of human socialization called "The Looking Glass Self," in which he argues that people develop their sense of self by observing how they are perceived by others. His theory written in the most succinct way possible is this:

> *I am not what I think I am, and I am not what you think I am.*
> *I am what I think you think I am.*

Our mind seems to construct a sense of self based on how others view us. The subconscious observes its environment then embodies its interpretation of it.

To illustrate just how permeable the subconscious is, there is a story of a very successful professional baseball player who while doing community work visits a prison and speaks to inmates. The prisoners were in awe of his visit. One prisoner asked the baseball player, "How did you become so successful?"

To that he replied, "I think it started when I was a child. I would always play catch with my father and he always told me I had an arm that would make millions. 'Keep throwing the ball like that son and you'll soon be signing a hundred-million-dollar contract with the Yankees' he'd always say," he continued.

"The same thing happened to me," one prisoner called out. Everyone turned around and waited for him to explain his claim.

"My father always told me I was too stupid for school. He told me I was going to end up in jail one day. My teachers said the same. And here I am."

The extreme permeability of our subconscious in allowing any and all stimuli to shape its nature adds to the urgency of becoming more self-aware. We need to tap into our *essence*. Our personalities, or who we think we are, are actually a function of our environment. When someone asks you *who you are*, you may reply with your name. You may mention where you're from and what you do for a living. All of these might describe you; however, they are not *you*. You did not choose your name or your hometown. As for your job, chances are you don't even care much about it and merely see it as another paycheck. We attach these attributes to our ego. Our bodily self. This is why we must identify our truest thoughts and discover our truest selves, and we can do this by attaining self-awareness.

The tug of war between the ego and our true selves demonstrates the importance of *intentional* deprogramming and reprogramming. Intentionality is key. As we discussed above, we cannot allow our comfort-loving, change-resistant subconscious to lead us down the journey of life. Our subconscious is merely an input of unvetted stimuli from those around us and not necessarily the character we wish to be. American entrepreneur Harley Davidson once said:

> *When writing the story of your life, don't let anyone else hold the pen.*

It's time to take the pen from your subconscious mind. You are conscious. An ever-deliberate being. You do not leave anything to chance. It's time to be hyper-intentional with everything you do, including that which your subconscious does.

Before committing yourself to the goals you have written for yourself, make sure these goals are your own and not a projection of society's expectation of who you are. Previously, we discussed reflection through journaling your past, present, and future. You learned how to use your past experiences to discover the *whys* of your current nature and to direct your future self with goals. But we need to refine this form of reflection further in order to gain clarity of who we really are.

Gaining self-awareness is the key to success in every field of life. It is important to know who you really are because you can only be happy by doing things that make the *real* you happy. If you continue to operate from your inputs, what society and the rest of the external world want you to be, you will conform to the perceived standards rather than to yourself. The standards of society are likely to be not aligned with your true self's nature. The state of society might even be antithetical to the nature of your essence. Which will cause you to live an uncomfortable life.

We have discussed the two different cognitive processes of the mind: fast and slow thinking. Then we related these two processes with two different states of mind: the subconscious and conscious mind. Where fast thinking is closely related to the subconscious state of mind and slow thinking is closely related to a conscious state of mind, two more concepts are related to these: ego and higher self.

# 5

# Your Thoughts Create Your Reality

*"If you change the way you look at things,
the things you look at change."*
—Wayne Dyer

I was addicted to the habit of negative thinking, similar to how one would be addicted to smoking cigarettes. I constantly felt the need to ruminate on my past. It's like I constantly had a natural impulse to think about all the mistakes I had made and how, if I had just done something differently, things could have been better.

I also was worried about the future and how the failures of my past only predicted incompetence in the future. I thought to myself I was only going to continue to make the same mistakes again. I think at the core, the reason I kept thinking about the past was I wanted to relive the experience differently, hoping that my constant thinking about it would change how it actually happened. Obviously, this was illogical, but as we have discussed before, we are not completely logical beings.

But the desire to feel better was not the only thing driving my negative thinking; I was physiologically addicted to it, just like a drug addiction, and you may be too. When we have bad thoughts about the past or future, our mind attaches emotion to that thought. That emotion comes up every time you think about that thought, and if it's a negative thought, it will be accompanied by a stress hormone such as cortisol. After thinking the same negative thoughts over and over again, I became addicted to the stress hormones and found myself thinking negatively more often. I was so focused on the bad in my past that it caused me to expect bad in the future. My negative thinking created a negative reality for me.

## Optimism is the new realism

*"Your beliefs become your thoughts,*
*Your thoughts become your words,*
*Your words become your actions,*
*Your actions become your habits,*
*Your habits become your values,*
*Your values become your destiny."*
—Mahatma Gandhi

The average human has about sixty-five thousand thoughts that cross their mind every day. And the vast majority, about 90 percent, of which are the same thoughts as the day before. Thoughts have two effects on your well-being:

1. Thoughts lead to beliefs, which lead to actions, which then dictate what you receive in life.

2. Thoughts create the environment of your body, which in turn dictates who you are.

Consider the concept of a placebo. When scientists conduct experimental trials to see whether or not a drug works in effectively treating a medical condition, they do so with a placebo group. This group receives a sugar pill, which contains no active ingredient. However, the recipients of this sugar pill do not know they are in a placebo group and instead believe they are receiving actual treatment. What's interesting is that occasionally, individuals who only take a placebo are cured of their illness almost as if they received actual treatment. The mere fact that you think you are being treated results in actual psychological and physiological changes in your body.

In his book *You Are the Placebo*, Dr. Joe Dispenza writes about a woman by the name of Janis Schonfeld, a forty-six-year-old interior designer living in California. She had been diagnosed with severe depression when she was a teenager and had been living with the condition ever since. Although her condition was so severe that she flirted with the idea of committing suicide a few times, she never sought professional help.

When she saw an ad for an antidepressant study at the UCLA Neuropsychiatric Institute looking for volunteer subjects for an antidepressant drug trial, she wanted in. She arrived at the facility and met with the researchers who told her all about the drug she was going to take and how the study was going to work. She took a brain scan and left with a bottle of pills to be taken, one a day for the next eight weeks. Just a few days later, she started feeling much better. She was excited because she thought the new drug actually cured her of her depression. She felt some nausea but she was told that nausea was a common side effect of the drug.

Eight weeks later when the trial concluded, Schonfeld was no longer suicidal and felt like a new person. When she came into the facility to meet with the doctors for the last time, they revealed to her that she never received any actual drug and was part of the placebo group all along. Schonfeld couldn't believe it. She thought for certain that the changes she experienced had to be the effects of a powerful medication. She asked the doctors to check again, and they confirmed, she was only taking sugar pills.

The only active ingredient Schonfeld received was a *thought*. The thought of the expectation that she was receiving treatment that was going to make her happy. And this seemed to be enough to change Schonfeld's reality for the better.

Another story of when thoughts created one's reality gives the phrase "scared to death" a less metaphorical hue.

Sam Londe, a retired shoe salesman from Missouri, went to see a doctor after having difficulty swallowing. The doctor conducted a series of scans and discovered that Londe had esophageal cancer. In the 1970s, where this story takes place, esophageal cancer was virtually untreatable and was considered a death sentence. This was made clear to Londe and his family, who had accepted his seemingly unavoidable destiny. A few months later when Londe was due for another series of health examinations, the doctor found that besides cancer, every other test came back normal. His blood tests and vitals came back with healthy results. Despite the healthy results, Londe had a morbid physical appearance and looked virtually dead.

The surprise came after Londe's death when an autopsy found very little cancer in his body, not anywhere near enough to be the cause of death. There was some cancer present in his liver and lungs, but none present in his esophagus, which was thought to be what killed him. Sam Londe didn't die because of the cancer; he died because everyone around him, as well as himself, thought the cancer was killing him. He succumbed not to a physical disease, but to the beliefs of his immediate environment.

The stories of Sam Londe and Janis Schonfeld demonstrate to us the power of our thoughts. Now, what if we could harness this power of the placebo at will? To make our thoughts create our reality intentionally. To heal ourselves using a placebo of our own conception.

# 6

# Neuroplasticity

*"Imagination is everything.*
*It is the preview of life's coming attractions."*
—Albert Einstein

As we can see from the stories above, a sincere belief in something can bring that thing to fruition. Thoughts can be translated to actual physiological changes. Once upon a time not too long ago in the scientific community, the view of having fixed characteristics dominated popular belief. Ideas such as genetic determinism—that the genes you were born with dictate every facet of your life, and you are a helpless victim to your genetic code—were taught to our future doctors in medical school who in turn propagated this message to the greater society. The belief in neuro-rigidity, which stands in contrast to neuroplasticity, teaches that the human mind is largely fixed, and things such as intelligence, personality, and happiness are unchangeable. Today, modern science rejects the narrative of neuro-rigidity.

This chapter will explain how modern science debunks these pessimistic notions of rigidity. In her book *Mindset: The New Psychology of Success*, Carol Dweck writes about two different kinds of people in the world: those with a growth mindset and those with a fixed mindset. Those with a growth mindset tend to be more successful at what they do, and more successful overall because they believe that everything about themselves can be improved. People with a growth mindset believe that no if not very few characteristics about themselves are entirely immutable. While those with a fixed mindset believe that they are as they are and there is little they can do to change themselves. Those with a growth mindset are more eager to try new things and ask questions because they sincerely believe that they can learn from their failures and therefore should not be afraid to ask dumb questions or take great risks. They understand that failure is instrumental to growth. This, in turn, spurs their self-development.

Carol Deweck writes, "Picture your brain forming new connections as you meet the challenge and learn. Keep on going." This is the attitude that is necessary for you to have when approaching this chapter. You need to sincerely believe in your ability to grow.

Now, I want to reiterate the role of the subconscious mind when it comes to growth. Since about 95 percent of all your thoughts come from the subconscious mind, you need to use that remaining roughly 5 percent that makes up the conscious mind to intentionally mold your more powerful subconscious mind. In his book *You Are the Placebo*, Dr. Joe Dispenza writes:

> *As long as you're thinking the same thoughts, they'll lead to the same choices, which cause the same behaviors, which create the same experiences, which produce the same emotions, which in turn drive the same thoughts—so that neurochemically, you stay the same.*

## Fixed Mindset

"Thats just the way I am"

"I am under the control of my genes and early development"

"I avoid challenges as failures run the risk of looking stupid"

## Growth Mindset

"Theres always room for improvement"

"Never underestimate the effects of hard work"

Challenges are necessary to grow, and failures are an opportunity to learn."

In effect, the nature of the subconscious mind makes sure we are always living our lives through the lens of the past. So that your past self is mediating every event your current self is experiencing. And your past self is conjuring up every thought that comes to your mind at any given moment. This is problematic when you are trying to change yourself because, by definition, you cannot change into something you already are.

To get a better understanding of the nature of your thoughts, it helps to understand the structure of your brain.

Your brain is made up of about one hundred million nerve cells called neurons, and each neuron is shaped in a way that allows it to communicate with its surrounding neurons. Depending on where the neuron is located, it can have anywhere between one thousand to one hundred thousand synaptic connections that link it to other neurons.

Every thought you have is communicated through neurotransmitters, where neurons fire through a specific pattern of neural networks to initiate a specific thought. Memories are mainly stored in the hippocampus part of the brain where a group of neurons firing in a specific way will recall past memories. All thoughts, including memories, are a chemical connection that is made by a certain group of neurons. And when we are recalling a past event or a thought we had before, we do so through activating that specific set of neurons.

When we learn something new we initiate a new set of neuron connections. Because we have never thought of that thought before, a new piece of information will spur a new network of connections that were never previously made before. Therefore when you learn something new, you are literally creating a new neurological structure in your brain. This is neuroplasticity.

Because the subconscious is made up of our past experiences, and 95 percent of the thoughts we have in a day are derived from the subconscious, we continually solidify those old connections. Every day you are living on autopilot, through an unintentional manner, you further crystalize your past personality. An uninterrupted stream of subconscious thought delivers a life of neuro-rigidity that is antithetical to growth. Neuro-rigidity merely further activates neural connections that have been made before and therefore will not help you grow but instead keep you the same.

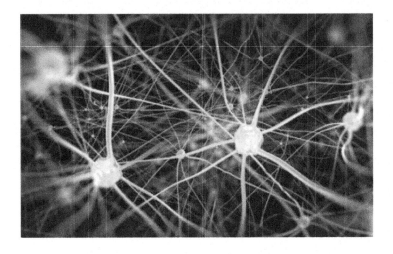

Neurons that fire together, wire together. This axiom holds true when we are speaking about the thoughts that occur in one's mind. If you continually have the same thoughts, you continue to reinforce the same thought patterns that make it more likely that you will have the same thoughts in the future. Dr. Dispenza elaborates on this further:

> *As your brain fires repeatedly in the same manner, you're reproducing the same level of mind. According to neuroscience, mind is the brain in action or at work. Thus, we can say that if you're reminding yourself of who you think you are on a daily basis by reproducing the same mind, you're making your brain fire in the same ways and you'll activate the same neural networks for years on end. By the time you reach your mid-30s, your brain has organized itself into a very finite signature of automatic programs— and that fixed pattern is called your identity.*

Ultimately, you are the architect of your brain. Every time you learn a new skill or a new piece of information you are carving out connections to shape your brain.

Neuroplasticity teaches us the importance of our thoughts in shaping our brains, thus shaping our personalities, and ultimately creating our reality. Our habits are also thoughts that continually shape our minds. Every bad habit that we are not putting a conscious effort to stop, prevents us from growth. Habits bring us closer to our past and further from our future selves.

I used the concept of neuroplasticity to my advantage when I was trying to change myself for the better. Our past has such an effect on who we are today. But the effect is not permanent. Although much of it happens below the level of consciousness, we can take the wheel and exercise conscious control over ourselves.

I exercised conscious control by learning new things. I read often. I also picked up new skills. I tried out different sports such as boxing and basketball. The skills and movements practiced in these sports were foreign to my brain and nervous system, forcing my mind to stay conscious and carve out new neural networks, exercising neuroplasticity.

The most impactful exercise I did was practicing meditation, and the ability to nurture the neural connections associated with positive thoughts and feelings. Meditation is the practice of mindfulness. Practicing meditation is to remain conscious in the present moment. Mindfulness helped me develop a form of mental control, to be able to silence my negative thoughts and worries. Most of the time, negative thoughts originate impulsively, below the level of consciousness. The more I meditated, the more I was able to control my negative thoughts and think positive thoughts.

The point of connection between neuroplasticity and meditation is promoting more positive thoughts and feelings, and less negative ones. Because meditation allows you to have more conscious thoughts, and conscious thoughts tend to be more positive, you will solidify the neural connections that are associated with positive thoughts and feelings, and weaken negative ones.

Being aware of my brain's potential to grow and change gave me hope that indeed I could change myself. That I was not a stagnant and rigid being. I could grow and change into a better version of myself. And that was what I set out on doing.

## Negative thoughts and toxic stress

During World War II, many skilled pilots who had proven their keen ability to fly fighter jets during peacetime oftentimes crashed their planes during battles. The heightened levels of stress that were absent in training overwhelmed the pilots' ability to successfully fly their jets. This spurred an interest in psychologists to find out why this happened. They concluded that the stresses of battle inhibit the brain's complex thinking capacities.

Now for those of you who are following from the previous chapters, complex thinking mainly takes place in the neocortex portion of the brain. This means that under stress, the body deactivates the neocortex and prioritizes more simple and instinctual behavior.

Negative thoughts trigger the release of stress hormones and place us in a similar mental state as fighter pilots in battle. When I was depressed and anxious, my mind never fell short of supplying me with negative thoughts, which in turn compulsively triggered stress hormones in my body.

The latest scientific research in psychology estimates that about 70 percent of our thoughts are negative and redundant. Like our friend Sam Londe who turned an internalized belief into his physiological fate, the effect that negative thoughts can have is surprising. Negative thoughts are physiologically different from other kinds of thoughts and are particularly detrimental because there is a heightened physiological reaction when we imagine the worst in our mind, namely the secretion of stress hormones.

First off, the mind has a negativity bias, meaning we are naturally inclined to think negative thoughts. This is likely because of evolution. Theoretically, when a human ancestor was roaming in the wild and they heard rustling in the bushes, if they imagined the worst, that a saber-toothed tiger with incisors the size of our ancestor's head was in the bush, their imagination would probably curb their curiosity and cause them to flee.

Thus the ancestors whose positive thoughts outnumbered their negative ones, and whose actions were guided by optimism, likely encountered more predators and other dangerous situations. The human ancestors who tended to think positive thoughts were more likely to be the predator's lunch. Depriving us of the blissful ignorance many of us need. Resulting in the modern human mind's tendency to catastrophize the unknown.

Today, this negativity bias does us more harm than good. While the risk aversion trait that is hardwired in our brains may prevent us from certain dangers today such as investing all our life savings into the stock market, it is not a sustainable behavior of thinking for modern Homo sapiens. Our ancestors may have been afraid of tigers and other predators, but today humans can fear practically anything and that is the problem.

We fear losing our job and stress about our financial situation. We don't want to see our marriages fail or worry that we may never find the right partner. News headlines are constantly reminding us of our mortality and the death rate of a raging pandemic. The twenty-first-century man and woman can be stressed about virtually anything.

Technological advances have transformed the way we live our lives and will continue to change the lives of humans. The human being does not adapt, biologically, nearly as fast. There is a growing divide between the world we have evolutionarily adapted to and the world of today. The asymmetrical relationship between humankind and the ever-advancing world gives rise to an over-stressed and over-worried population.

Our mind reacts to negative thinking by releasing stress hormones, and too much of these stress hormones are toxic to the mind and body.

When you have a negative thought, you trigger the limbic system of the brain. The limbic system is responsible for emotion and attributing value judgments. A thought is not "negative" until your limbic system perceives it to be. Since every thought is a firing of neurons in a specific way, a negative thought that is repeated is further solidifying that pathway and making that thought more significant. The more you revisit that thought, the more prominent that the neural pattern that comprises that thought becomes.

Negative thoughts trigger stress. There are three main stress hormones your body releases when you are stressed: adrenaline, norepinephrine, and cortisol. Studies show that when the body releases stress hormones in excess, it negatively affects the brain and body. This is called *toxic stress*.

Stress hormones are released in the body to help you in life-threatening situations which, according to evolutionary theory, looked like escaping that potential tiger that might have been hiding in the bush. Adrenaline, which is known as the fight or flight hormone, will prioritize the body's survival capacities such as those of the lungs and muscles to aid in fighting or running. This means the body will allocate energy away from non-survival faculties and to the parts of the body needed to survive that situation. Cortisol, another stress hormone, has a similar effect. This results in the virtual shutdown of the prefrontal cortex, which is a portion of the neocortex responsible for more complex cognition, as well as other parts of the neocortex.

When negative thoughts trigger a stress response, precious metabolic energy is rerouted away from the prefrontal cortex, which is the location of higher-order thoughts. Creativity, compassion, and love are all compromised as the prefrontal cortex struggles to perform at normal capacity. Firepower is instead allocated toward locations in the brain where simpler cognition takes place such as the limbic and ganglia portions. Heightened activation in the limbic system during stress leaves the limbic system excited and more easily aroused.

In sum, constant stress has a long-term structural effect on neurons located in many parts of the brain. I want you to focus on only two of the effects of stress on the hippocampus and the prefrontal cortex. The hippocampus has a major role in learning and memory. This makes the hippocampus essential for creating new thoughts and firing new neural pathways. As discussed previously, the prefrontal cortex is the seat of complex thought and therefore consciousness.

Damage caused by negative thoughts and the subsequent release of toxic stress to the hippocampus and the prefrontal cortex will hinder efforts of reaching higher states of consciousness and achieving self-mastery. Thus it is imperative to minimize negative thoughts and emotions so that the stress response and the negative thoughts themselves do not affect the structural makeup of your brain in a way that will inhibit your ability to grow.

## *Fake it till you make it*

*"I am the greatest, I said that even before I knew I was."*

—Muhammad Ali

He wrote a $10 million check for himself, marked "For acting services rendered," and dated it ten years from that day. At the time he wasn't happy with the kind of work he was getting and knew he deserved better. This is not a story about some check fraudster; this is another account of Jim Carrey.

In 1985, a broke and depressed Jim Carrey drove his beat-up Toyota to the top of the Hollywood Hills. He dreamed of success and to be able to finally find the kind of acting job he felt was right for him. On that Hollywood hill that evening, he wrote himself that $10 million check that would change his life. He placed it in his wallet where, as the days went by, the check deteriorated more and more. Almost ten years later, in 1994, Jim Carrey was paid $10 million for his lead role in the comedy film *Dumb and Dumber*.

During a 1997 appearance on the *Oprah Winfrey Show*, Carrey explained why he symbolically wrote that check for himself and placed it in his wallet.

> "*I would visualize having directors interested in me and people that I respected saying, 'I like your work,' and I would visualize things coming to me that I wanted ... and I had nothing at that time, but it just made me feel better*," Carrey shared.

*"I wrote myself a check for $10 million for 'acting services rendered' and I gave myself 5 years ... or 3 years maybe. I dated it Thanksgiving 1995 and I put it in my wallet and I kept it there and it deteriorated and deteriorated. But then, just before Thanksgiving 1995, I found out that I was going to make $10 million on Dumb and Dumber,"* he added.

Carrey visualized his success before it even happened. He imagined what he wanted his future to look like. He imagined film directors complimenting him on his work. Carrey then wrote a physical check. This reflects how confident he was in the belief that he was going to be a successful actor. Carrey's thoughts attracted his reality.

Some call it manifesting; others call it using the law of attraction. Whatever you want to call it, the act of visualizing your future self is powerful. The idea of manifesting has a bad reputation because it may seem silly. Some question how visualizing something in your head has any causal linkage with getting an actual outcome. This is a warranted concern, but the problem is how many have attempted to explain manifesting, which I will try to do a better job at.

Just as Jim Carrey did, to achieve what you want in life you first must know precisely what you want. Once you know what it is specifically that you want, visualize yourself having it. You need to imagine yourself already being the person you want to become. Imagine your future reality in the present. This is how you can best guarantee your future outcome.

Your current life is a carbon copy of your subconscious beliefs. What you struggle with in life indicates that your subliminal programming does not allow for that thing to actualize. And what you find yourself so easily attracting is made possible because of a belief you have.

For example, if you are struggling with finding a stable relationship partner, you need to look inwardly and find a self-limiting belief that you may have. A belief that is ingrained within your master program that you might not have been aware of. It might be a belief that you are not worthy of having a partner or marriage. At a deep level, your sense of self may only allow for the possibility of having casual or mediocre-style relationships. You may have been raised in an environment where there were no people involved in serious relationships, so you never identified with the kind of people who do have them. Or you may have been so interested in the relationships of celebrities that you involuntarily inculcated your sense of self with that style of short-term dating.

Whatever the belief is, you need to identify it and replace it with a new belief that supports your goals in life. Through reflection and meditation, you can be more aware of which programs help or hurt your cause. I will discuss meditation in the following chapters.

When I was broke, depressed, and practically paralyzed, I used visualization to help me get to a better place mentally and physically. Doctors told me it was likely that I would never fully recover, and not be able to run again. At the time I was also addicted to pain medications, which were prescribed to me at first but that I became addicted to later on.

I visualized myself as a strong and healthy athlete, able to do all exercises. I visualized myself running, jumping, and playing football. I then conjured up images in my head of me as a real estate investor, a published book author, an active contributing member of the community and I imagined myself starting a small business as a fitness trainer, using my passion for fitness to help other people reach their fitness goals. I could go on and on about the details; I even created a vision board, but what was important was that I imagined it first from a place of sincere conviction and belief.

Then I added a feeling of gratitude for having what I wanted even though I hadn't received it yet. I was grateful for having what I visualized. Gratitude is a high-level emotion. Thoughts are powerful but when a thought is charged with a feeling or emotion, it becomes even more powerful. Because I gave my visualization the emotional charge of gratitude, that visualized thought left a greater impression on my mind.

Thirdly, I brought that visualized thought into physical form by words, small goals, and actions. This could be in the form of writing yourself a check and placing it in something you see every day like a wallet, such as Jim Carrey did. For me, that meant writing down my goals in specifics and always going back to them. I revisited what I had written every morning after I woke up and before I went to bed. Writing my goals down helped me see clearly what I wanted and put the rest of my day in perspective relative to that goal, and I looked at every interaction I had with the world as a means to achieving that goal. That way I would always be on the lookout and never let an opportunity slip past me.

I also reminded myself of my mission through vocal affirmations. I told myself I was a successful real estate investor. I also told myself I had a healthy and strong body. I affirmed these beliefs over and over and over again.

I then detached myself from the outcome and lived as if I was that person with those habits. I did not worry about it not happening; instead, I stayed positive and was convinced it would happen. I just had to be patient.

Lastly, I worked my butt off to get to where I envisioned myself being. I would go for a walk until, eventually, it was a jog, then a run, then I was able to go to the gym. I would then make time to study real estate every day while I was working full-time. I created small, realistic goals that would lay the foundation for my bigger goals. In sum, the four main steps are:

1. Visualize using mental imagery what you want your future self to look like. Use words in the present tense such as "I am" instead of "I will be." Use detailed imagery.

2. Express a heightened emotion toward that visual, preferably the feeling of gratitude.

3. Bring the thought into the physical world by writing it down and constantly reminding yourself that you are your future self.

4. Detach from the outcome and focus on the positive.

5. Work for it.

We know visualization works because studies show that your mind does not differentiate between imagined experiences and actual external experiences. It cannot tell the difference between what is happening to you and what you think is happening to you.

In one experiment, two groups of non-pianists were asked to learn one-handed piano exercises and to practice two hours a day for five days. The difference between the two groups was that one group actually practiced using a physical piano and the other group practiced without moving their fingers; instead, they just imagined themselves practicing.

After five days, brain scans showed that both groups grew the same amount of new brain connections. These findings suggest that the mind does not know when you are imagining an experience and will even change its structure to more closely conform to what it believes it is doing. A belief in something can change your physiological state to support that belief. We can use this to our advantage.

Since the thoughts we have shape our neurology by creating new pathways, the thoughts you have when visualizing your future create a map of the future in your mind. You are creating those new pathways and every thought you have of your future self further enforces that specific pathway, which makes it more likely that you will think of that thought again.

So, if your past thoughts and experiences have shaped your present subconscious belief systems, which have created your present reality, and your present beliefs will create your future reality, therefore, it makes sense to intentionally shape your belief system now. By creating a mental image of yourself in the future, with great imagery and detail, you are telling your mind that is who you are and all your programs should support that personality. Your subconscious will oblige and slowly change its paradigms to advance the character it thinks it is.

You need to attach an emotion to that visual to make the thought more dramatic in effect. Emotions bypass the conscious mind and activate the limbic system, which is part of the subconscious mind. Because the aim is to reprogram the subconscious mind, we need to speak a language that the subconscious specializes in, which is emotion. The conscious mind is too critical of a thinker; that's why we need to circumvent it using emotion. And not just any emotion; it needs to be a heightened emotion. There are many elevated emotions, of which gratitude and love are by far the highest. Being thankful and expressing love in the present moment for that which you visualize to happen in the future, will lead your mind to believe that you have already received that which you visualized. The figure below diagrams states of emotion and orders them from highest to lowest.

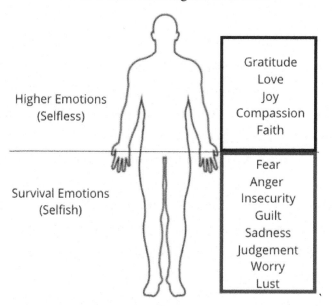

Higher Emotions
(Selfless)

Gratitude
Love
Joy
Compassion
Faith

Survival Emotions
(Selfish)

Fear
Anger
Insecurity
Guilt
Sadness
Judgement
Worry
Lust

Jim Carrey's check was placed in his wallet, something he opens daily, and every time he opened his wallet he was reminded of his purpose, to get that $10 million role.

The check symbolized to him what his ultimate goal was. You need to do something similar. For me, it was simply writing down my goals on paper. I revisited these goals every morning and every night before I went to sleep. American author Sir John Hargrave once said:

*Until it's on paper, it's vapor.*

There's something about having a physical stimulus that makes your goals more palpable. Once it's on paper, your subconscious is more aware of your direction, and when seen enough times, the subconscious will construct a paradigm that conforms to those goals.

I also repeated affirmations aloud to myself. Since the subconscious mind takes in all sensory input, you need to consciously slip in the input that you want using affirmations. These are positive and goal-oriented sayings you repeat to yourself with the intention of it slipping past your conscious mind and being absorbed by the subconscious.

The beauty of affirmations is you can say anything you want and over time your mind will mold to the meaning of what you are saying. I started every morning by saying "I am grateful for my life and I am improving the things in my control, I am grateful for my life and I am improving the things in my control, I am grateful for my life and I am improving the things in my control." This was just one of the many affirmations I said. I also said goal-specific affirmations. There are certain times in the day when your subconscious is most responsive to affirmations because of the brain wave state you are in.

I will discuss affirmations and brain wave states further in the following chapter on meditation. For now, just understand that to leave a more impactful imprint on the subconscious, you need to turn the thought into something physical such as writing it on paper and saying it aloud.

You need to detach from the outcome. Have you ever bought a new car, say a Mercedes Benz, then noticed that so many people drive a Mercedes? It's almost as if everyone decided to buy the same car after you bought yours. Clearly, that's not what happened. What happened was because you have invested in that type of car, and see your car every day, you are more familiar and attentive toward that kind of car. Now you are unconsciously more responsive whenever you see a Mercedes as opposed to, say, a Toyota. It's not because there was a significant increase in the number of Mercedes-Benz cars on the road, but that whenever a Mercedes happens to drive by you, you are more likely to notice it.

Similarly, by focusing on the positive, you will always be on the lookout for opportunities that will help you reach your goal. If I had worried about not reaching my goal, I would have been saying negative things to myself such as, "What if I fail and waste all this time?" This will make me unconsciously more attentive toward when things go bad and discourage me, which will attract the negative. But because I detached from the outcome, it allowed me to stay positive. By staying positive, I was able to focus on all the things going right while striving toward my goal. This helped me stay confident in myself.

Your confidence in yourself will increase substantially once your internalized beliefs coincide with creating your future self. You need the help of your subconscious mind. You cannot try to muscle through using only the conscious mind because the subconscious is more powerful and will surely defeat you. Your visualized thoughts, when done enough times, will begin to replace the old beliefs that have been holding you back. The more negative beliefs you replace, the more confident you will be.

The benefits of being more confident cannot be overstated. You perform better and think clearer when you are confident in your abilities. Confidence will lead to fewer thoughts of self-doubt, less negative thinking, and less worry because you trust yourself enough. You don't have to worry about not achieving your goals when you are confident because you know you will succeed. This leads to less anxiety and stress. Confidence leads to competence, which will bring about the things you want in life. It will make all the things you want statistically more likely to happen.

Confidence also increases your motivation to act. The "what if" thoughts will be outnumbered with "I got this" thoughts, and your fear of failure will subside. This will substantially increase your desire to execute your plan and work for what you want. You will be more resilient. You will be better able to see your weaknesses and look at them objectively instead of being defensive about them. You can work on your weaknesses and effectively improve yourself.

Confidence will allow you to live a more authentic life. You will stick to your principles and not care about what others think. Because you love yourself enough, you won't depend so much on the approval of others. Therefore you will act according to your own will and not what you think others want. This will help you live a more principled life, which will attract others whose values resemble your own. All of this will increase the likelihood of becoming your future self.

Finally, you need to work for what you want. At the end of the interview with Oprah, Jim Carrey said:

*Visualization works if you work hard. That's the thing. You can't just visualize and go eat a sandwich.*

In typical Jim Carrey fashion, he adds a humorous tone but the message is simple; you need to use the power of visualization in combination with working hard. The mental work is in the visualization. The physical work is putting in the hours and taking actionable steps to achieve what you want.

When you "fake it till you make it," your mind doesn't know that you are faking it and actually thinks you already made it. The belief that you "made it" will develop into more beliefs that support the future self that you envision yourself being. A sincere belief in yourself is crucial to actualizing and attracting your future self. The more your subconscious believes that you are your future self, the more confident you will be in acting out who your future self is. The more confident and motivated you are, the more likely you will become the person you want to become.

To summarize, the logic of visualization is as follows:

1. Your mind cannot differentiate between imagined reality and actual realities.
2. Imagine your desired future self in detail and in the present.
3. Your subconscious will replace beliefs that created the current you with beliefs that conform to the visualized, future you.

4. You will attract what you visualized because you are now unconsciously focused on the parts of life that support the goal you are trying to achieve.

5. Thus, you are more likely to accomplish the goal of becoming your future self.

# 7

# Rituals of Change

*"We first make our habits,*
*then our habits make us."*
—John Dryden

I spent several years living a lifestyle of drugs, alcohol, and casual sex, coupled with depression. It's crazy how fast that kind of behavior clings to the ego. Girls loved cocaine so I always kept that around. I made so much money selling it that I kept a part-time job just so no one would get suspicious about how I was affording my lifestyle. The money generated from selling drugs allowed me to do whatever I wanted. I partied every night, which meant every morning I woke up with a hangover from all the drinking the night before. I also often woke up next to a woman I didn't even know the name of.

A lifestyle like that brings with it a feeling of emptiness. The consistent dopamine rushes might lead you to believe that you're enjoying yourself. However, those sources of momentary pleasure cannot be mistaken for happiness. In fact, it results in the complete opposite. You look back at it and can't help but feel depressed. Depressed because you gave years of your life to fleeting pleasures without any real productivity. Depressed because, intuitively, you know that drugs and casual sex are not good for your soul. Not only are they physiologically damaging but spiritually as well. The latter being hard to explain in words because the feeling is so innate. It's almost natural that, despite your body craving dopamine, your mind knows its toxicity.

The depression I had developed induced within me a habit of negative thinking. This is a terrible habit to have. I found myself constantly ruminating about my past. I was reliving my worst experiences. I thought about my ex-wife leaving me and another man stepping into my daughter's life. I thought about the death of my mother a lot. These thoughts came with emotions. Feelings of guilt and blaming myself for all the problems in my life. Feelings of hopelessness brought me to believe I couldn't do anything about myself. It made me believe I was hopeless. In short, I was a prisoner of my thinking. I was a slave to my habit of negative thinking.

Fast forward a few years to right before I set out on my self-transformation, along with the habit of negative thinking, I was addicted to pain medication, cigarettes, and my subconscious longed for me to return to my drug-dealing days.

Reflection brought me face-to-face with my habits, and since habits are a direct reflection of my programming, that is where I began. The first step to changing who I am was to change my habits. Today I do not drink nor smoke. I do not do any drugs and as I am writing this, I am on the path to a stable marriage. I wake up before sunrise every day and exercise daily. I was able to change myself by developing good habits, what I call rituals of change.

When I was on my transformational journey, a necessary step that preceded deprogramming and reprogramming myself was the ritualization of six actions. Self-reflection, which I have introduced already. Meditation, positive self-talk, physical exercise, diet, and prayer. These six can be broken up into three general categories in which they directly affect either the mind, body, or spirit, as shown in figure 2.0 below. Each individual ritual is connected to all the others in a way, either directly or indirectly affecting all three elements of being.

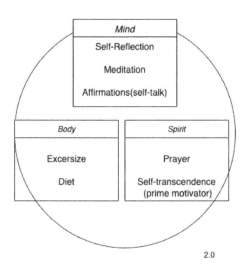

2.0

We are slaves to our habits; that is why we must have only good habits. A habit is a thought or behavior that is repeated so many times it becomes second nature. It is a manifestation of your subconscious mind. It is a direct command from your programming, usually unmediated by conscious thought.

## Meditations, not medications

*"Meditation is not about stopping thoughts, but recognizing that we are more than our thoughts and our feelings."*
—Arianna Huffington

In a world where advertisements tell you what you should want, where television suggests how you should act, and where society tells you what you should do, how do you know what *you* want? How can you separate the external stimuli from your internal essence? What makes matters worse is we now carry around small screens that constantly collect data about us to make it easier for big corporations to manipulate and profit off of us. Historian and philosopher Yuval Noah Harari once said:

*In ancient times having power meant having access to data. Today having power means knowing what to ignore.*

We need to block out the noise and listen to just ourselves, and we can do this by practicing *mindfulness*. We spoke about reflection and how you can find yourself through retrospection into your past and setting goals for the future. However, the flaw with reflection is how do you know that the goals you set are actually your own? How do you know that your perception of the past and current interpretation of it is the interpretation of your true self?

Today, we are so constantly bombarded by information, that we confuse other people's opinions with our own. After all, we know how amendable the subconscious mind is to external stimuli and how quickly ideas stick to the subconscious.

Motivational speaker Jay Shetty illustrates how he was able to silence society's demands and amplify the voice coming from his true self. Shetty explains that when he was younger he always wanted to be an investment banker. Everything was going according to plan. He studied hard and graduated from a top finance school.

Gradually, he stopped and asked himself why he wanted to be a financier in the first place. He looked at the way investment bankers were perceived in his community. He took note of how his community equated success with the financial means investment bankers seemed to have. He then realized it was not he who wanted to be an investment banker, rather it was his community that wanted him to be one. And by growing up in that community, he had drifted into its expectations of him.

Society indirectly exercised agency over him, and while he thought it was he who desired a career in banking, that desire was exogenous in origin.

Jay Shetty has a fascinating story that you'll have to read more about in his book, but suffice it to say that after he made this realization, he devoted his life to service by becoming a monk, and now a motivational speaker. He is now doing what he wants to do instead of what society wanted him to do. Interesting right?

So how do we get in tune with our true thoughts? One solution is meditation.

Meditation is the central act of self-awareness. All change starts with the mind and meditation is the act of taming the mind. Meditation allows one to step outside their programming and think from the conscious mind. Once you are thinking from the conscious mind, you can more clearly see which thoughts come from the conscious and which come from the subconscious.

You are also creating more conscious thought, which is more deliberate and intentional. You are living in the present when your thoughts are deliberate. Your conscious thoughts are a better reflection of your true self while the thoughts that stem from your subconscious are a reflection of your past experiences. Practicing mindfulness through meditation allows you to detach from your ego, fundamentally changing the way you relate to your emotions and lower forms of thought. The more you practice thinking from your conscious mind, the more focused you will be.

The goal of meditation is to
1. prolong your conscious, deliberate thinking
2. observe your unintentional programs
3. shift the way you (conscious mind) relate to your feelings(subconscious) and essentially dial down the intensity of your emotions
4. identify your truest thoughts.

When you meditate, you are attempting to put your subconscious on pause. You are taking control of your mind by silencing your inner voice that just doesn't shut up. You are stopping all thoughts, both conscious and unconscious. When water is calm and still, it becomes visually clear. When that water is running, it becomes hard to see through it. This is analogous to how the mind responds to meditation. Meditation makes your mind calm, like still water, allowing us to see things clearer.

Sixty-five thousand thoughts slip in and out of the average human mind every day, and roughly 95 percent of those thoughts happen below the level of consciousness. The vast majority are compulsive and involuntary in origin. The more thoughts that originate against our conscious effort to silence them indicates how little control we have of our minds. And since our thoughts ultimately control our reality, when we have little conscious control over our own thoughts, we inevitably have little control over our own lives. That's what meditation seeks to solve. Psychologist and author Fyras Elsebai describes meditation:

> *[Meditation] is reconnecting with our true inner self—freeing the mind of consistent negative thoughts and restlessness.*

I'm sure you've heard about the many kinds of fancy-sounding meditations and I hope that hasn't intimidated you. But at the very core, all forms of meditation have a central theme: to be grounded in the present moment. I know that sounds a bit vague especially since everyone in the mindfulness community seems to throw that phrase around without really explaining it. What it means is to pay attention to your breath and let all other thoughts slip past the mind. Refrain from deliberate thoughts and try your best to silence the unintentional voice. Since the unintentional voice stems from the subconscious, and the subconscious is a record of your past, when you are in the present you are in complete consciousness.

This is why mindfulness may seem a little uncomfortable at first. Because we have become conditioned to expect that subconscious mind to supply us with a steady stream of thought, trying to turn it off when you are meditating is effortful for the beginner who finds it hard to calm their mind. After a couple breathes into meditation, their autopilot regains control over them and before they notice, they are hundreds of thoughts deep into rumination and worry.

## Presence is bliss

> *"Yesterday is history tomorrow is a mystery but today is a gift that's why we call it the present."*
> —Eleanor Roosevelt

Meditation trains you to stay in the present, which means you are experiencing life in the *here* and *now*. When you train your mind to stay present in meditation you are building the habit of presence to permeate into every aspect of your life. Because meditation is the act of complete presence and consciousness, you are building the skill of mindfulness that will make you present throughout the rest of your day. Presence means you are noticing the texture of the book you are currently reading rub against your fingertips. You are aware of the lighting in the room and how it's making you feel. Living in the present moment implies not thinking about the past or worrying about the future, because the past and the future are by definition not the present. Chinese philosopher Lao Tzu said it succinctly:

*If you are depressed you are living in the past.*
*If you are anxious you are living in the future.*
*If you are at peace you are living in the present.*

Sometimes we are tempted to live in the past because we feel like we can think our way out of a bad decision that already happened. This is obviously illogical since the past has already passed. Everybody, even the most successful people, can dwell on how doing things differently in the past could have resulted in a better outcome; however, this is a poisonous act because this type of thinking more likely than not will lead to negative thoughts spiraling out of control and into a depressive episode.

We are also tempted to constantly worry about the future. Thoughts about the future are also skewed negatively and more often than not turn into fears. The mind catastrophizes potential situations, blowing them way out of proportion. This is what the Roman philosopher Seneca was referring to when he famously said:

*We are more often frightened than hurt;
and we suffer more from imagination than from
reality.*

The bulk of our suffering is imagined because we refuse to live in the present moment. We escape the present and find refuge in the past or future. When one is uncomfortable with who they are they try to avoid coming face-to-face with themselves.

Meditation brings you face-to-face with who you are. By silencing the noise, and tuning into the present, you are plugging into the conscious mind. In such a state, you are now able to observe yourself from a third-person perspective. You are detaching from the subconscious, emotional, ego. You are identifying only with the conscious, which only exists in the present moment. The mutually exclusive relationship between past and present, and subconscious and conscious, correlate respectively. You become the observer.

When you detach from the ego, you are in a better place to recognize which part of you operates from your programs and which part is your actual essence. Through this process, you are attaining self-awareness. Meditation allows you to know yourself better by identifying which are your truest thoughts, your conscious thoughts. What thoughts have been drilled into your head by your environment and which thoughts are endogenous, a product of your own conception?

By detaching from the ego, you are detaching yourself from an automatic emotional response, and are more deliberate in the reaction you give to the events around you. The lower forms of thought that originate from the limbic and reptilian parts of the brain become less impactful on you the more you meditate. When you meditate you are training your mind to be deliberate with every thought, so that less impulsive thoughts arise. Since compulsive thoughts are filled with emotions such as fear, guilt, and worry, you are training your mind to have fewer negative thoughts. The result is a more constant stream of uninterrupted thoughts originating at the conscious level, the seat of rational and complex thought. This allows you to think more clearly and live less on reactive, survival-mode thoughts that lead to a fearful and brutish life. Earlier in the discourse, I introduced a quote by Victor Frankl that read:

> *Between stimulus and response there is a space.*
> *In that space is our power to choose our response.*

We are programmed to have socially conditioned reactions to events, as well as evolutionarily developed behaviors that compulsively dictate how we respond to the world around us. When we meditate, we become aware of these programs and come to the realization that every event is made up of three distinct elements: the event itself, what we think of the event, and our response. No event should automatically trigger any response, as an event and the response we give are not necessarily related to each other.

The great hallmark of being human is exercising free will (to some degree) and having the ability to control our instinctive urges. We share many characteristics with animals and one of which is having automatic and unconscious thoughts that lead to action. For animals, their thoughts are rigidly correlated with their actions, meaning their actions are almost entirely instinctual and without rational thought. Aristotle said that the essence of a human being, and what distinguishes the human from the animal, is rational thought, to be able to do or not to do. To have an internal dialogue within themselves and exercise calculated actions. As humans, we must capitalize on our ability to be rational and deliberate. That calculation is found within the event-response gap.

Meditation makes us aware of the event-response gap and makes us question assumptions. It helps us recognize and prolong the gap between an initial thought or feeling and our reaction to that thought or feeling. This leads to less reactive thoughts and moods, thus allowing us to live deliberately with happier thoughts that we intentionally control.

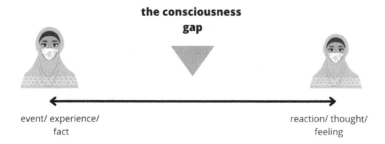

the consciousness
gap

event/ experience/
fact

reaction/ thought/
feeling

Scientific research backs up the effect of meditation on the mind. fMRI brain scans were performed on experienced meditators and first-time meditators to see the difference in neural pathway activation between participants in the two groups. The scans show that experienced meditators exhibit lower activation in the prefrontal cortical midline structures and language-related left inferior prefrontal areas. These areas are associated with negative self-talk and worrisome chatter. So a decreased activation in these areas indicates someone who is more comfortable with themselves.[1]

The brain scans also revealed a decreased activation of the amygdala, which is part of the limbic system of the brain and is responsible for triggering a stress response. A less active amygdala correlates with less cortisol and adrenaline secretion within the body, which are hormones that cause a toxic stress effect on the brain and body. A more relaxed amygdala is also associated with less negative thoughts since negative thoughts tend to trigger the limbic system, which in turn releases a stress response.

Another scientific study shows that meditation seems to thicken the prefrontal cortex, which is the location of complex and rational thought. Researchers used magnetic resonance imaging to assess the cortical thickness of meditators and non-meditators. The results found that meditators, compared to their controls, had significantly greater structural thickness in the neural pathways associated with empathy, attention, and sensory processing.[2] We can reasonably infer that meditation develops higher forms of thought. And since the prefrontal cortex can be considered the control panel of the mind, the stronger the neural connections present within the prefrontal cortex, the more control we have over our minds, thoughts, and the rest of our lives.

It is important to build a habit of meditation so that you do it every day, and not only on days that are convenient. If you depend on motivation to get you to meditate, you will find days where you lack motivation. If you build a routine of meditating and include it in your daily schedule you will find yourself more consistent. A routine trumps motivation.

## You are what you eat

Being ultra-deliberate about your life means taking control of every detail, including the way your body looks and the food you allow to enter your body. I was not confident in my appearance. I didn't like the fact that I had more tattoos on my body than a socially outcasted '90s biker gang member. I didn't like my height, my weight, and even the way I looked. I realized that how I feel about myself is also how the world will feel about me.

Humans have developed the remarkable ability of emotional intelligence. We are able to get a sense of how others feel. It is like an advanced form of empathy. We can figure out when someone is happy or sad. We can dig deeper than the outward display of smiles and frowns. More reliable indicators such as eye contact and body language stem from below the level of consciousness and outside the realm of awareness, giving us a better idea of how someone is feeling. Word cues and the specific language used by a speaker also happen outside conscious control. Finally, the overall atmosphere, or the "vibes," someone may give off allows us to have a better understanding of their emotions.

I was unhappy with myself. I was not comfortable in my own body. I let my insecurities shadow all the good, and all I could think of were my negative features. In short, I hated myself, and it seeped through. I had no confidence in myself, and others knew. It was written on the walls of every room I walked into. The natural ability of emotional intelligence relayed my discomfort to everyone around me.

My own lack of confidence was read by those around me, and they responded with their own lack of confidence in me. My own self-hate was read by those around me and they responded with their own hate toward me. It is another example of a self-fulfilling prophecy. It is also another example of the law of attraction.

So before I could go out and conquer the world, I had to start by conquering my mind. I had to build my confidence. I needed to love myself so that the world can love me.

My subconscious beliefs were convinced that I was a failure. It has concocted a mental framework of belief that I was not to be taken seriously. Thus the first step was to overcome that belief. We know that beliefs come from the subconscious level of the mind. Meditation allowed me to do that which was explained above. Secondly, I built confidence in myself by loving the way I looked.

You do not necessarily have to work out to love the way you look, but that is how I did it, and it worked for me. I went to the gym every day and worked on my body like an artist on their sculpture. Chipping away every day. Every day after the gym felt like a day well spent. A day when I worked out was the epitome of "carpe diem," to me, and gave me a sense of accomplishment. A sense of working toward my dream body. And in the grander scheme, another step toward my goal of self-transformation. This gave me a sense of satisfaction, which translated to self-love. Sincerely loving yourself is the source of all confidence.

Self-love is important because when you have a love for yourself, you feel sufficient in yourself, thus you are not so reliant on the love you receive from others, or their validation and approval. Your source of love is innate, stemming from within. Only when you are relying on your own backbone, can you feel free to express yourself the way you really want to. Only when you have a sufficient amount of self-love will you do the things you want and say what you want to say knowing it might not be in the interest of someone else. You won't be afraid to ruffle any feathers because your source of love is from within and under your own control.

I cultivated self-love by creating the body I wanted. I did this by spending countless hours in the gym and by being very meticulous about my diet. I ate only high-quality foods. I did not allow myself to consume processed foods or any food that would counter my goal of achieving my dream body. Eating only high-quality foods also has a psychological element in that when you eat high-quality foods, you feed into a high-quality sense of self. When you eat well you feel well, which makes you act well, and others act well toward you. There are certain foods that when consumed, elevate your stress levels. As stated previously, a stress response triggers negative thoughts. And since your thoughts create your beliefs, and your beliefs create your reality, eating foods that will increase your stress response leads you to a negative life.

Gone are the days when eating meat meant going to the local farm to pick up some freshly slaughtered beef along with a hand-milked jug of cow's milk. When cows roamed freely in an open field and grazed on the grass side by side with other cows. Back when farmers had the patience to allow their animals to grow naturally, without injecting them with any growth hormone in an attempt to boost profits. And when getting milk meant the farmer's kids would gently rub the female cow's back to comfort her while another would gently pull on her udder pouring her milk into a bucket. This picture of a family-operated farm stands in sharp contrast to agricultural practices today.

Factory farms dominate the agricultural industry. Ninety-nine percent of all animal products in the United States, such as beef, chicken, pork, eggs, and milk, come from factory farms.[3] For those of you who do not know, factory farms are exactly what they sound like. In a factory farm, animals are treated only as a commodity whose value is only derived from a cost-profit analysis. Where profits are paramount and empathy is costly. Cows, for example, are kept in an unnatural state, indoors, where they can't even conceive what the brightness of the sun looks like, let alone ever having seen it. Cows raised for beef and milk are crammed together with little wiggle room. Compared to cows raised for veal, that little amount of wiggle room is a dream. Cows raised for veal, in order for their flesh to stay soft to the human teeth,

112

typically spend their entire lives placed in twenty-two-inch by fifty-eight-inch crates. They will never in their lives be able to take three consecutive steps in either direction. Cows in factory farms sit sloshing around in their feces and urine until some mechanical contraption is supposed to pick up after them. Cows have their tails surgically removed so that they don't get in the way of the mechanical milker trying to make its way to their udders. Oftentimes, this pseudo-surgery is done haphazardly and without any anesthetic, causing chronic pain to the cows. Cow udders, much like human nipples, are soft and when the rough material of the milking machine comes in contact with the skin, it causes pus-gushing blisters that spill into the milk to be ingested by the consumer, and of course puts the cows in further pain.

This story is the dominant paradigm for all factory-farmed animals and not just cows. Chickens, for example, are packed like sardines, one on top of the other in cages, where the lower the chicken is placed in the cage the more unfortunate its fate is when nature calls for the chickens above it. I can go on and on. The theme here is that 99 percent of animals raised for consumption are in a constant state of stress. Like humans, when animals are in pain, they release a stress response consisting of cortisol and adrenaline. When animals are in constant pain like overcrowded conditions and bodily injury, these stress hormones flood their blood and find their way into the muscles and flesh.

When anxious animals make their way to the slaughterhouse, and finally on our dinner plate, we ingest the traces of cortisol and adrenaline. These stress hormones make their way into our bloodstream, making us stressed. We then think negative thoughts because we are stressed, strengthen the neural pathways of those negative thoughts, and are thus more likely to trigger our own stress hormones.

Ingesting stress hormones will also decrease immune function and place you at greater risk of many kinds of diseases such as heart disease and hypertension. When researchers fed piglets orally administered doses of cortisol, the stress hormone concentration in the piglet's blood increased as well.[4] The piglets subsequently showed a decreased ability to fight off infections, therefore supporting the notion that the stress hormones present in the meat we consume will cause and increase the stress hormone levels in our bodies. Furthermore, surgeons typically inject stress hormones into an organ transplant patient when receiving an organ to weaken the patient's immune function so that their immune system does not attack the transplanted organ.

Besides the fact that there are harmful traces of stress in the animal products we consume, there are other reasons why the overconsumption of meat is hurting you. Meats are loaded with saturated fats that build up as cholesterol in the arteries and increase your risk of heart disease. A simple Google search can uncover the endless list of health risks that come from eating meat. I wanted to mainly discuss the risks associated with stress because I believe that the stress induced by meat consumption is understudied, which is indicated by the fact that it will not result in a symmetric Google search.

This is not a case to go vegan, as there are still nutrients present in meat that are not present elsewhere. Plant-based diets have their own drawbacks such as not providing a sufficient amount of fats that the body needs to regulate hormones. Plant-based foods are often soy-based, which also disrupts the body's regulation of hormones, which increases the likelihood of a greater stress hormone concentration in the body. These diets also have difficulty sourcing iron and vitamin D, which can induce a depressive mood. And the list goes on. The message is that either extreme, too much meat, or too little of it, is not a good thing.

The solution is the middle ground: Structure a diet that works for you, with meats and animal products in moderation. The majority of your plate should be derived from plant-based sources. Meats are necessary because they have proteins, vitamins, and fats that are difficult to derive from solely plant-based foods without compromising some of your health.

Almost everyone is aware that exercise has significant health benefits for the human body, but few are aware of the effect it has on the human brain. Exercise is very similar to meditation in reducing stress and promoting the robustness of the prefrontal cortex. When we exercise, our heart rate increases, and more blood flow reaches the brain. This increases the amount of oxygen and other nutrients that reach the brain, promoting greater health for each neuron.

Have you ever gone for a jog and felt like you can go for a few more miles? If so, you've probably experienced a runner's high. A runner's high is a sense of euphoria that brings about a feeling of calmness and relaxation to the athlete caused by a series of neurochemicals and endorphins being released in the brain. When performed regularly, exercise changes the structure and behavior of the brain.

Motivation is needed to act and change in our lives. All actions come first from thoughts, but what induces that thought that leads to action in the first place? It is a neurochemical called dopamine, that serves as a motivator for action. When we lack a sufficient amount of dopamine, we feel lazy and lethargic, with no motivation to act in any way. Regular exercise increases the circulating levels of dopamine and dopamine receptors in the brain.

Regular exercise also reduces stress. Exercise positively affects serotonin levels in the brain. Serotonin stabilizes our mood, feelings of well-being, and overall happiness. More serotonin and dopamine responses make us feel happier and induce a positive outlook on life. Instead of looking at life negatively, regular exercise will help you focus on the positive.

Exercise also builds up your capacity for presence. Athletes have long known about the extreme levels of focus that bring the athlete into a heightened state of consciousness called "the zone." This is a state where all worries flee the mind of the athlete when they are focused on one thing: the immediate goal at hand. This is akin to a thoughtless meditative state with respect to mastering the mind in the present moment.

You need to focus on diet and exercise to see effective change in yourself. The food we eat provides the building blocks for our cells, which are the building blocks of the biological unit we call the human body. If we are eating processed foods and meats from animals that are in a constant state of stress negativity, through digestion and absorption, we will embody that characteristic of negativity. The profit-driven nature of the modern agricultural industry creates a dismal environment for its livestock, that live in a state of chronic stress to the point of morbidity.

The stress and negativity associated with factory farm animals persist when those animals are converted to food products such as meat, milk, and eggs. When we consume these products, we are also consuming that stress, which will manifest through us. A diet with moderate meat portions will not only provide you with enough protein and nutrients needed to live a healthy life but will also express a sense of empathy and compassion toward animals. Empathy and compassion are complex forms of thought that occur in the neocortex region of the brain.

When we meditate we develop these regions so it is important to apply these high states of emotion as much as we can and since factory farming is a very cruel practice by any objective standard, reducing our consumption of meat is a moral obligation. We hope that an awareness of the effects of factory farming encourages the adoption of better living conditions for the animals, and management in the industry trades some of the value placed on profit with a sense of humanity.

The effects of regular exercise on the brain are hard to overlook and are similar to the effects of meditation. Exercise makes us happier and less stressed. Thus, on the journey to change yourself, you need to stick to a strict diet and workout plan.

# Part Three

# 8

# All of This Is Found in Islam

*"Allah has a purpose for your pain,*
*a reason for your struggles,*
*and a reward for your faithfulness.*
*Don't give up."*
—Dr. Bilal Philips

What took me the greater portion of my life to discover, I found in the teachings of Islam. I had been searching for guidance on how to lead a meaningful life and found all the answers in this beautiful belief. Now if you're not religious, I want you to bear with me for a moment. For now, you can substitute God with the *universe* if you're agnostic, *probability* if you're atheist, and so on. I want you to read the following with an open mind because you do not need to adhere to any specific religion to benefit from this message.

What may be a literal truth may as well be a metaphorical truth, meaning while I may believe in the literal presence of God, the heavens, and His angels, I may not be able to convince you of their existence. The next best thing is to convince you to *act* as though God, the heavens, and His angels are in existence. Thus, while I maintain a literal belief in my faith, and you maintain a metaphorical one, there may be no substantial distinction in the way we interact with the world and with ourselves. So if you do not manage to find a place in your heart for a direct belief in what I mention in the following, I hope you arrive at the next best place, a sincere embracing of these ideals.

I was born a Muslim but I did not inherit the religion. My father was a very spiritual man. He was born and raised in Egypt before he came to America. When he was living in New York City he would rarely ever miss the Friday prayer at the mosque. He stayed disciplined with his five daily prayers throughout the week and would read the holy Quran often. After my mother and father divorced, I lived with my mother and her new husband, George, who was an atheist. George was the aggressive type of atheist, not the kind who shrug their shoulders and say, "I don't know and don't care" when asked about their thoughts on religion. No, George was hostile toward religion, not just an atheist but an anti-theist. I remember one time when I was a child, my brother and I were speaking Arabic with one another after picking up on the language while living in Egypt.

"What the fuck are you two saying? You will only speak English in my house!" George screamed at the top of his lungs.

He was visibly angry as if we had committed a crime by speaking Arabic. I never spoke Arabic in that house again and ended up forgetting the language. Another instance happened after I had asked my mother not to include pork in our family dinner as I couldn't eat pig meat because of my beliefs. George found out and purposely bought pork for my mother to cook. George offered twelve-year-old me an ultimatum: "Either you eat pork like a normal person or you're not eating at all!" Living in George's house stripped me of my religion.

Years later, after spending many years living on my own, I had virtually lost my faith. I did not pray regularly; I drank, did all kinds of drugs, and had casual relationships with women. But during my journey of self-transformation, I rediscovered Islam. All the pains, suffering, losses, and heartaches led me to the doorstep of Islam.

I started this book with a discussion on suffering and I want to come full circle. I stated that the world left me hurt and I was looking for answers. I couldn't fathom why my mother was murdered along with my baby brother and sister. And I definitely couldn't understand why a so-called omnipotent God who had the power to stop it all, didn't. Instead, He sat back while George went on a video game-like killing spree that left me and my brother with immense psychological baggage that I carried with me for years to come. After all, the Stoic philosopher Epictetus once argued:

> *Is he [God] willing to prevent evil, but not able? then he is impotent. Is he able, but not willing? then he is malevolent. Is he both able and willing? Whence then is evil?*

So why should I, or anybody who has suffered in this world, believe there is a God? Why should I, when I know my family was murdered, there's endless bloodshed in wars, many starve to death in famines, and heck, there's even bone cancer for children? These are valid questions, and although I know God is in control of all, and thus the cause of all my suffering, I love God so much that words can never be able to describe my love for Him. My love for Him is not a case of Stockholm Syndrome. It's because it was through my own suffering that I was able to find the answer to life's biggest mystery. Let me explain.

## Suffering in Islam

> "When life brings you to your knees, you're in the perfect
> position to pray."
> —Rumi

On December 14, 2012, a twenty-year-old man named Adam Lanza walked into an elementary school in Sandy Hook, Connecticut, armed with an AR-15 assault rifle, two pistols, and wearing a military vest. Earlier that year the school principal ordered a new security system installed in the building, which required all visitors to be visibly identified and buzzed in. Lanza used his assault rifle to literally shoot an entrance into the building. Upon hearing this loud "popping" noise, the school psychologist and assistant principal went to investigate; only one of them would survive.

At about 9:30 a.m., students heard a mixture of announcements over the loudspeaker and sounds of gunshots. Students were rushed into bathrooms and closets by teachers. The gunman made his way from one classroom to another. In one classroom, a female teacher ushered her students to the back of the room, away from the door. Lanza forced his way in and shot her. Six students were killed in that classroom alone. By the end of the day, twenty students all under the age of eight, along with six adults, were killed by the gunman before turning the gun on himself.

News of this horrific incident spread all over the world. People were devastated. Some were quick to blame the gun and others the gunman. All, however, asked the same questions: How could any human do this? And more importantly, how could God allow this to happen to innocent children?

This question brings to mind Fyodor Dostoevsky's novel *The Brothers Karamazov*. In the novel, Ivan is an intelligent young man who can't quite embrace faith in the same way his brother Alyosha, who is a novice monk, does. It's not because he didn't like the rules set on him by Christianity; it was because he couldn't reconcile the suffering in the world with a loving God such as the one described in

124

the Bible. In a moment of honesty, Ivan tells his brother, "It's not God that I don't accept, Alyosha, only I most respectfully return him the ticket." Ivan had heard stories of children too young to know what evil was, let alone be afflicted by it. He couldn't understand why a loving God would allow things like the Sandy Hook Elementary shooting to happen. "Listen," Ivan says, "if everyone must suffer in order to buy eternal harmony with their suffering, tell me what have children got to do with it? It's quite incomprehensible ... therefore I absolutely renounce all higher harmony. It is not worth one little tear of even that one tormented child who beat her chest with her little fist and prayed to 'dear God' in a stinking outhouse with her unredeemed tears!"

Ivan has a point. When writing about suffering, why should I include the only entity who can stop it all? Why should I mention religion and God in the same book meant to help you get through suffering when God is seemingly the cause of all worldly suffering? Theologians have tried to answer this question in the past with a rather insufficient answer: God is not the cause of suffering; suffering is caused by our own free will. This is no help. This fails as an answer for many reasons, one of which is because much of suffering is due to natural causes such as earthquakes and famine, and not because someone willed to harm another. So, what is the answer? If God loves us, why does He cause us so much pain?

The first answer is we don't know. Long before Ivan, Nietzsche, or any other skeptic asked the question of suffering, this question was asked by the angels. The Quran narrates:

> *And (remember) as your Lord said to the Angels,*
> *"Surely I am making in the earth a successor." They*
> *said, "Will You make therein one who will corrupt in*
> *it and shed blood while we extol (with) Your praise*
> *and call You Holy?" He said, "Surely I know what*
> *you do not know."*

—Quran 2:30

Here, the Quran is narrating a conversation between God and the angels, in which God announced His plan to create a "successor," meaning humans on earth. The angels responded in a very indirect manner: Why would You create a corrupt and violent creature? In other words, why create humans that will cause evil and suffering? Allah (swt) responded not by answering the angels' question, but by saying He knows the reason why but they don't, implying there is wisdom behind His decision; however, not everyone comes to know this wisdom. By replying He knows what they don't, Allah (swt) is tacitly saying there are reasons for creating humankind that outweigh the angel's concerns about bloodshed and corruption, but that knowledge is withheld from them.

Everything written in the Quran is written intentionally and by the best of writers. Every character, every event, and every story—including this conversation—was written for us to draw lessons and learn from. So we do not know nor are we meant to know why suffering takes place on the earth. We have to realize that Allah (swt) is communicating that to us through the words of the Holy Quran. And maybe there is beauty in not knowing why something bad has happened to you.

Indeed I believe there is: It puts your mind, and your heart, at ease. Knowing that God, the one who created you with the intention of creating exactly you. By knowing you are not the product of a dice roll gradually evolving over a long period of time, rather you are the calculated creation of intelligent design, you can calm your nerves and put your trust in the divine. Everything happens by the will of the One who created you. Nothing is an accident. The Quran illustrates Allah's (swt) extreme attention to detail with the verse

*Not a leaf falls except that He knows it to be.*
—Quran 6:59

Every leaf that falls from a tree is intended to fall at that exact time and to land in a prespecified place. So why is it that we think the bad things that happen to us are actually bad when everything that happens to us is the result of divine intention?

In sum, the first answer to why we suffer is simply that we don't know. And we do not need to know all the *whys*. Since suffering will always exist here on earth, the best we can do is to lessen the pain and we can do this by trusting that God wants the best for us and His master plan is ultimately guided out of love. All the ups and downs in between are part of the journey to which only He knows why each one is there.

Now you might say that is not an answer. You might argue that simply not knowing why we suffer is insufficient to lessen the pain we go through. And you may be right. But there's more to it.

It is communicated through the Quran that God is The Most Loving (*al-Wadūd*), so why then does He cause suffering? Does He not *love* the children who are starving or the ones who serve as collateral damage in countless wars? Indeed He is The Most Loving, but God is also described in the Quran as The Most Wise (*al-Ḥakīm*). To have wisdom means to know things that not many others know about. This is confirmed with many verses attributing knowledge of that which is concealed and unseen (*ʿIlm al-ghayb*) to Allah (swt) only. The Quran says:

> *No one in the heavens or the earth knows the unseen except Allah.*

> —Quran 27:65

All the bad in the world, the suffering, and the evil are instrumental to the actualization of God's plan, rather than being an intended outcome. The bad is, in some sense, a means to an end. Only God knows exactly why you are going through the things you are going through. The best we can do is to have trust in His wisdom because He knows what we do not.

I have found that a perspective shift, from reasoning and to faith, is key to leading a happier life. The constant need for answers stems from the desire to control, which at the root comes from the low emotion of fear. In contrast, faith requires trust, which at the core comes from the higher emotion of love. When you have faith you are at ease, and make peace with whichever outcome unfolds. You expect good and emanate positivity. On the other hand, when you are anxious about the future, you do not trust that the desired outcome will unfold. This is unwanted for two reasons, both of which we have discussed earlier. One relates to the concept of our thoughts creating our reality through the causal link of a self-fulfilling prophecy. Namely that expecting a positive outcome will manifest a mindset of optimism, confidence, and creativity, which will increase your chances of achieving your desired outcome. While being worried leads to pessimism, less confidence, and less creativity, as explained in the earlier chapters.

Oftentimes, we worry and stress about the things we are going through, not knowing the reason why we are going through them instead of placing our trust in God because we want to have complete control over every part of our lives. I want to, for a moment, revisit the topic of control and fate. Like I have mentioned previously, most of the time control is good and we must be intentional with certain matters such as in choosing the people we associate with, the goals we set for ourselves, our habits and daily routines, and so on. We must try our best to control the things we can control. But there are parts of our lives we cannot change. We definitely cannot control the past and should spend no time trying to. However, the grey area between the things within our control and the things outside of it is preparation for an outcome. We are not able to control whether or not it rains on the day of your big job interview, but you can check the forecast. You cannot completely control the outcome of the interview, but you can check all the boxes by heading there extra early and spending more time preparing for the interview. That is where your focus must be. The outcome is in your hands only insofar as the things you can do. Concern yourself only with the internal goals of doing your part, and not of the external goal of getting the desired outcome. Because ultimately, no matter how hard you try it is possible that you fail.

Keeping this in mind, without a belief in God's divine wisdom, one is inclined to stress about the events in their life because they don't believe in intentionality and wisdom behind every effect. The believer has the advantage of optimism. They believe in the intelligent design of the universe, and thus the intelligent design of all their life events. They immerse themselves in the maxim that everything happens for a reason. While the exact reason is not clear, that is beside the point. The immense feeling of optimism brought about by a belief in divine decree need not be explained by logic and reasoning because logic pales in comparison to faith when it comes to making one feel better and feel loved.

A sincere belief in the power of God's decree (*qadr*) will erase any regretful thoughts about the past and any anxious thoughts about the future. When you believe that the One who created you and loves you is in control of everything around us with extreme precision down to every quark in the universe, there is no need to worry.

Earlier, I have written that through retrospection of your past events, the things we once thought to have been bad in our lives, sometimes aren't bad when put in perspective of the bigger picture. I told a story of a king who became so upset when he sustained an injury he berated his best adviser. Later on in the story, it was revealed that his injury would have been the sole reason why he remained alive. The lesson from this story brings comfort to those who are going through a rough patch or feel like things aren't going as they planned them because it teaches that there may be good in the things you perceive to be bad. There may be blessings disguised as misfortune; it also may be that something you thought you really wanted turns out to be something that you are better off without; only time will tell which is really which. But for the faithful, everything that happens to you is good because the believer is convinced that everything is by the will of God, who only intends good. God writes this beautifully in the Quran:

> *Perhaps you dislike a thing but it is good for you, and perhaps you like a thing but it is bad for you. God knows, and you do not know.*
> —Quran 2:216

This powerful verse from the Quran reminds us to accept the bad with open arms and to not be stubborn about what we think is good for us. It asserts our vulnerability as humans. It reminds us of our infallibility, that we may be wrong. It also reminds us of who is never wrong, which is God. Assuring us that there is no need to panic because ultimately we are in good hands.

The following story illustrates the concept of *tawakkul* (trust in God's plan) quite well. In 1979 a Syrian man arrived in the United States, a completely foreign land to him, and he felt completely foreign to that land. Shortly after he settled in his new home in California, he booked flights for his wife and seven children to join him in his new country.

Their flight itinerary from Damascus included a mandatory stop in New York City, where all immigrants were to be vetted and documented by the proper authorities at the time. This was followed by a stop in Chicago to finally catch a connecting flight to Los Angeles, their final destination. When they arrived in New York, one of the daughters, Hala, who had recently put on a hijab in observance of her faith, was told by authorities to take it off for her photo, but she refused. For those who don't know, a hijab is a covering worn by Muslim women as an expression of modesty and faith. Immigration officials consistently told her she needed to remove all head coverings for the photo, and she wouldn't be able to enter the country or board her next flight until she took the photo.

Hala's mother became impatient. Having traveled halfway across the globe and spending virtually their entire life savings on plane tickets, she began to worry about missing her flight or being sent back to Syria. She urged and pleaded with Hala to simply remove her hijab and take the picture. Hala stood her ground. Officials continued to reason with her but she wouldn't budge; she told them no matter who you bring, I will not remove my hijab. Hours and many supervisors later, they acquiesced and allowed Hala to take her photo with her scarf on. However, by then, it was too late. Their connecting American Airlines Flight 191 had already departed without the family on board. They had to purchase new plane tickets and stay overnight in New York. This financially burdened the family even further. The mother was angry at Hala and up until they arrived in California, the mother lectured Hala about what she did.

When they finally arrived at the Los Angeles airport, the father greeted them with tears and a big hug.

"I can't believe you're alive! Praise be to God you're alive!" he screamed.

"Of course we're alive; why wouldn't we be?" they asked.

"The original flight you were supposed to get on crashed, and everyone on it died," the father replied.

Being delayed by authorities saved their lives. Although it seemed like Hala's encounter with the authorities was bad by any objective measure because she was flirting with the possibility of being sent back to Syria, it turned out to be the greatest thing to ever happen to her. It was impossible to foresee that missing her flight was actually a good thing. It was not until after knowing the fate of American Airlines Flight 191 could anyone be able to say with certainty that missing their original flight was actually a good thing. I cannot read minds, but I think it goes without saying that Hala trusted Allah (swt) that things would work out. She did not worry about missing her flight because she knew Allah (swt) was ultimately in control of what happens. She saw that staying true to herself was more important than worrying about whether or not she was going to miss her next flight.

That is the kind of trust we need to have. To be comfortable expressing our true selves without worry, concerned only about what Allah (swt) thinks of us.

When we have tawakkul we perceive everything that has happened as a manifestation of Allah's (swt) wisdom. We might have wanted something else to happen, but we must be grateful for whatever Allah (swt) decreed. Allah (swt) knows what we do not know, so we can never for certain say whether not getting that job was a bad thing or missing that flight was bad. What we do know for certain is that everything is by the will of Allah (swt) so we must appreciate the wisdom from which that will operate. Imam Al-Ghazali took this a step further when he famously said:

*There is not in possibility anything more wonderful than what is.*

Al-Ghazali is explaining that the way the world is, is in fact the best it can ever be, because everything in the entire universe was created, planned out, and executed by a perfect and divine being; therefore, it is perfect. Al-Ghazali believes that all the evil and pain in the world is not intrinsically bad, but is only perceived as bad by people; instead, Al-Ghazali explains that all bad leads to a greater good. A net positive that is unrealized at the moment. A soon-to-be mother goes through nine months of aches and pain from the physical discomfort of carrying her baby inside her; however, she doesn't call it suffering. She also goes through hours of onerous contractions until the baby comes out. Yet despite the pain, she would do it all over again. When the baby arrives she doesn't hate the baby because of the immense pain it has brought. Instead, she loves her new child. The pain is there, but it is instrumental in order to achieve a greater good, the baby. For many mothers, having a child would be described as the best thing that has ever happened to them. This is the point Al-Ghazali is trying to make in regard to the bad in the world. We should not focus so much on the bad things that happen to us; instead, we should understand the bad as a stepping-stone, a lesson, a transitory experience bringing us to a better place, much like the pains of labor bring a woman to the honorary status of a mother.

Still, you might say that the possibility that all bad may lead to a good does not explain why God must include pain and suffering in the world. You may not find that reason to be compelling enough.

To that, I agree. But there's more and we have to go even deeper. And I'm going to avoid the "without bad, how can there be good?" argument. Not because it's not true, but because it is too obvious. After all, what would a perfect world look like? Let's go beyond the surface.

Indeed, the blame for our suffering does rest on God. He causes it and can stop it at any moment if He wills to. But this suffering is not in vain because, while we may be able to love without suffering, we do not love if we are not willing to suffer.

To love something necessitates the willingness to sacrifice for the sake of that thing, and sacrifice, oftentimes, is in the form of pain. I may say I love my wife, but if I'm not willing to sacrifice something, say part of my income or my Friday nights for the sake of our marriage, then do I really love her? If not, then it is certain that I don't love her enough to make those sacrifices. We often hear stories of parents taking on two, even three jobs so that their child can have a meal. These are sacrifices made by the parent out of love. Similarly, if we turn away from God the moment something bad happens, then do we really love God? If you are resilient in your faith despite the pain that you know was caused by the very being your faith requires you to love, that is true love. To be able to maintain our divine love despite the pain and suffering that we go through is the ultimate good.

The act of giving up something you *want* for the sake of something greater is the ultimate form of love. This is what Islam is all about. To surrender our immediate wants for our divine love. To discipline our fleeting whims in an endeavor for ultimate success. And if we lose our faith the moment something we don't want to happen, happens, then how robust is our faith? How much love for the divine do we really have?

The best way to prove our love is by sacrifice, by enduring pain, and by staying persistent in our faith.

We express our love for the divine by recognizing the good that we have been blessed with and not letting the things we perceive as bad overshadow it. Our minds may have a negativity bias, in that we give greater attention to the bad than an equal degree of good; having faith means we give greater weight to the good because we expect good. Having faith means focusing on the good and be patient with the bad. Having faith means showing acceptance to whatever fate God has decreed upon you because you know that all that comes your way, every experience, event, and outcome is the unraveling of the Creator's plan.

## Faith helped me get through tough times

*"Death has nothing to do with going away ...*
*the sun sets and the moon sets, but they're not gone."*
—Rumi

In the tumult of the year 2020, I lost my father to the coronavirus. In the early days of the pandemic, COVID-19 spread like wildfire through the densely populated neighborhoods of New York City. My father, Mohammed Mashaal, after complaining about trouble breathing, found out he had been exposed to the coronavirus while at work. Soon after, he would lose his battle with the infection and pass away.

For several years, I lived with my father in his NYC apartment where we bonded. During that time, we underwent spiritual and character growth. After learning of my father's death, I was faced with yet another tragedy; I was grieving the loss of a parent once again, all with the backdrop of a worldwide pandemic. And to top it all off, I was fighting my own battle with the coronavirus, which I got from my father in my last few moments with him in the back of an Uber on our way to the hospital.

Stress is when you feel like the pressure from an external demand far exceeds your capabilities of dealing with it. I felt overwhelmed. When I lost my father, all the stresses, from my mother's death to my father's, seemed to hit me at once. I felt like part of my old self was whispering to me, telling me to give up and that all my efforts were going to waste. My old self bombarded me with negative thoughts such as that I was going to die from the virus. My lower self was filling me with fear, trying to convince me that my lungs would eventually collapse from the viral infection.

But I fought back. I effortfully moved my thoughts to a positive space. I knew that my thoughts would affect my body's ability to fight the virus. If I believe I will succumb to the disease, my body will believe it as well, resulting in my immune system losing its willpower and being less effective in fighting the virus. This is why I stayed optimistic and tried to think only positive thoughts.

I was now left to face the reality of my father's death, accepting it as part of my fate. The Creator's timing is perfect because all the growth I had experienced, the habits and behaviors I had taught myself prior, protected me from falling into hopelessness. It was almost like a timely transition, from years of character and spiritual development to being thrown into an ostensibly dark place of mourning and despair. My father passing away put my self-development to the test.

I realized through embracing my earlier suffering that I could do this again. I can control my emotional states by accepting the outcome and focusing on what is in my control. I protected myself from lower desires and thoughts of illness by praying often and remembering that this life is temporary and all things pass. I am not saying this was easy. I did slip up. Many of us will slip up at times as we are not perfect. But I was reminded of my bigger goals and I was able to catch myself. Remembering Allah (swt) and being God-conscious centered me. Remembering to be grateful for all that I was blessed with helped me be patient; as we know gratitude and patience go hand in hand. I held to my conviction that " I am today what my thoughts were yesterday," and like I said early in the book, I decided to live by the fact that I am a victor and not a victim.

I was not able to attend my father's funeral except by a Zoom video with all my relatives from around the world. The graveyards in the New York area had no availability so we buried him in a graveyard in Maryland. I was not able to see my father's gravesite until a couple of months after his death. This was a very hard time for me. I went from taking my father in an Uber to the hospital, to accepting the fact he was six feet underground, all within the span of a few days. It all happened so fast that, at first, I was overwhelmed with sadness and denial.

However, Islam was the guiding light that brought me from this dark place of grief and fear to a place of love, acceptance, and contentment.

Firstly, by remembering Allah (swt), I was able to cope with all my stress. The year 2020 was a time of uncertainty. The future was not certain, and for many people, being in a state of uncertainty and unpredictability can be frightening. They cannot close their eyes and have faith. While I wasn't in any better position to predict the future than most people, I did have certainty in one thing, in Allah (swt). Allah (swt) says in the Quran:

*Verily, in the remembrance of Allah do hearts find peace.*

Certainty and faith are somewhat antithetical. Faith is a belief in the unseen, beyond the boundaries of evidence. In contrast, certainty is belief beyond any doubt. Certainty offers a sense of security and predictability because you can know what's going on. People tend to desire certainty because it feels safe.

I had an unshakeable belief in Allah (swt). I was certain of His presence and provision. I was God-conscious, and this led me to accept all that happened to me, and all that the future has in store for me. I did not know for certain what will happen to the world, but I did know that it is in Allah's (swt) hands. From a place of certainty, I accepted uncertainty, which dispelled any fears I had.

Secondly, my awareness of Allah (swt) was reinforced, multiple times throughout the day every day, by being on top of my daily prayers. Self-help gurus and millionaire mentors obsessed with materialistic gains tell you to "maintain your relationships and nurture your connections with others" because "your net worth is your network." This is sound advice but how often are we nurturing our relationship with the Creator? How often are we developing our connection with Allah (swt)? Prayer is how I maintained and nourished my connection with the Creator.

Being strict on myself with my prayer seeped into every sphere of life. Being disciplined with your prayers develops the underlying character trait of conscientiousness and overall willpower. Maintaining *salat* is the result of overall self-control and discipline. That is why the Islamic caliph and companion Umar Ibn Al-Khattab once said:

> *Hold on to your salah, because if you lose that, you will lose everything else.*

Salat increases your level of discipline because it requires a degree of self-mastery to perform the prayers and do them on time, aligning the body and soul toward a single goal. Salat increases your focus because similar to a state of meditation; you need a constraint stream of focus during prayer. Both discipline and focus are crucial to keeping you in the present moment.

While enduring the psychological pains of losing my father, I was inclined to slip up. I had impulses out of my conscious control telling me to drink the pain away. To just have a good time and snort some cocaine. The evil tendencies of my lower mind tried their best to convince me to mask my pain with pleasures. The very first impulse was to miss my prayer. To not offer salat because I'm in pain, or so my lower mind reasoned.

However, I did not give in. Salat was my guard. I fought off the lethargic demands stemming from my lower mind by being strict with my prayers. The heightened level of consciousness, especially awareness of Allah (swt), brought about by maintaining salat was what kept me stable. The focus and discipline practiced in salat developed in me a level of self-mastery that I used to stay on the right path. I was able to successfully avoid destroying my life because of the despair of death a second time. I did not allow myself to sabotage all that I have been working on for the past several years.

Islam saved me. Islam taught me the personal character and habits I so desperately needed to successfully cope with the death of a family member. I can say this with confidence because I can look back at how I dealt with death when I didn't have a firm holding of Islam. My first experience with death was a tragedy, not only because of the murder of my mother (may God have mercy on her) but because of my reaction. I spiraled into an aimless life of drugs, alcohol, and depression.

In comparison, my second experience with death, losing my father to the coronavirus, was completely different. I had a firm foundation. My bedrock was a firm belief in Allah (swt). My pillars were the pillars of Islam, and that had made all the difference. The robust way of life offered by Islam helped me grieve the loss of my father.

## Hopelessness is a sin

*"Indeed, with me is my Lord;*

*He will guide me."*
—Quran 26:62

Moses did not know that God was going to split the sea for him. All he knew was that God was not going to abandon him. Immediately behind him and his people were Pharaoh and his army who had been following them for miles, wanting to capture and enslave them, while killing many in the process. They were severely outnumbered and ill-equipped for battle; to any reasonable person, this situation was imminent doom for Moses and his followers. However, did Moses lose hope? Absolutely not.

> *And when the two companies saw one another, the companions of Moses said, "Indeed, we are to be overtaken!" [Moses] said, "No! Indeed, with me is my Lord; He will guide me." Then We inspired to Moses, "Strike with your staff the sea," and it parted, and each portion was like a great towering mountain. And We advanced thereto the pursuers. And We saved Moses and those with him, all together. Then We drowned the others.*
>
> —Quran 26:61–66

Moses had no idea how he was going to make it out of this situation. What he did know for certain was that Allah (swt) was with him and was not going to abandon him. He had unshakeable certainty in the power of the Almighty, and even when he was backed into a corner, seemingly without any chance of escape, he did not, for even a moment, despair in the plan of Allah (swt). He and his people put in the effort to get to the Red Sea. The effort was on him, but the outcome was up to Allah (swt).

Unshakable faith and optimism go hand in hand. The story of Prophet Moses teaches us to never despair in the hope of Allah (swt). To always expect good. To stay optimistic and not worry or stress. We say hopelessness is a sin in Islam because it comes from a lack of faith. It comes from a nihilistic outlook on life. When you have faith that Allah (swt) is in charge of all affairs, you cannot help but stay positive.

Let us ponder on the beautiful names of Allah (swt).

## *Gratitude and patience are the two halves of faith*

> *"So be patient, with a beautiful patience."*
> —Quran 70:5

The latest research in psychology overwhelmingly finds gratitude to be paramount in living a happy life. Gratitude and patience are central in Islam and found all over the Quran and sunnah. Islam has a beautiful way of communicating the importance of patience and gratitude, by detailing how the prophets behaved in times of hardship. The most beloved people to walk this earth lived lives of pain, hunger, betrayal, and all other kinds of discomfort unimaginable. On the other hand, some prophets were not tested as much and lived lives of relative comfort. What is common among all of the prophets is they maintained their faith in God by displaying two virtues: *Sabr* and *Shukr*. There is no English equivalent for these concepts but the closest that comes to Sabr is best characterized by the two English words, patience and endurance. And Shukr is best translated as gratitude.

The Prophet Muhammed ﷺ was born in one of the harshest places in the world, the Arabian Desert, to a very harsh people and culture, a time so backward that it was named the "Era of Ignorance." He was born into a life rife with struggle and heartache, yet he retained the most beautiful character. It was for this reason the Pakistani poet Mohammed Iqbal said:

> *Sure you can deny God, but how do you deny*
> *Muhammad?*

Comparing where he came from to how he was, it is clear that the Prophet Muhammed ﷺ was special. Modern sociology tells us we are the product of our environment; however, a case study into Muhammed's life flies in the face of this theory. Muhammed was a beacon of light in the darkest place of the world. He spread his light to all those around him by teaching in turn, transforming Islamic civilization into a source of light unto the rest of the world. When writing the book *The 100: A Ranking of the Most Influential Persons in History*, Michael H. Hart placed Prophet Muhammed at the very top, in first place, and defended this ranking by saying:

> *My choice of Muhammad to lead the list of the world's most influential persons may surprise some readers and may be questioned by others, but he was the only man in history who was supremely successful on both the religious and secular level.*

Despite his struggles, Prophet Muhammed always showed patience and was never discouraged by adverse circumstances. Muhammed was born an orphan who never saw his father. At the age of six, his mother died. He remained under his grandfather's supervision until he passed away when Muhammed was only eight years old. This is just a glimpse of his painful childhood. It was a very hard time for him but he always kept a positive attitude. Throughout his life, he had to encounter a succession of bitter experiences. No parent should ever have to experience the burial of their child; Muhammed buried seven of them. During his life, he lost all his children except one, Fatima. He also witnessed the death of his beloved wife Khadeejah. A companion of the Prophet stated he often saw Muhammed spend the entire day suffering from hunger and the Prophet often could not find even the worst dates with which to fill his stomach. His wife Aisha said that many times there was nothing to eat in the Prophet's household other than dates and water. For months on end, no fire would be lit because there was no need to cook what wasn't there. Despite all his suffering, Muhammed stayed faithful in God's mercy, patient in His plan, and grateful for everything.

Many of the most revered personalities struggled just as we do. We can find commonplace between the lives of the prophets and other Quranic characters and with our own struggles. Adam went from literal paradise to losing it all. He subsequently lived an earthly life of adversity until the day he died. Despite his leadership, Noah's own son rejected his message, teaching us that even when we do our best in raising our children they still may not turn out the way we want. After losing his son, or at least he thought he did, Jacob wept until he went blind. Moses and his people were made into refugees by Pharaoh, forced to travel distant lands risking their lives on the voyage. Today, many migrants lose their lives trying to find safe lands. Mary was a single mother, in a society trying to shame her for being who she is, and Jesus, the son of Mary, oftentimes did not have shelter, except the wilderness and lived in poverty, reportedly using a rock for a pillow. The world has transformed greatly over the past decade, let alone since the times of the prophets; however, many things do remain unchanged. Their lives parallel our own. We learn a lot from the stories of the prophets, but one overarching theme is that they too suffer. The Quran says:

> *We shall certainly test you with fear and hunger, and loss of property, lives, and crops. But [Prophet], give good news to those who are steadfast.*
>
> —Quran 2:155

The prophets having a harsh life is indicative that God's wisdom includes testing those He loves. Just ask yourself this question: Why would God decree a harsh life, instead of an extravagant one, on the very people He entrusted to represent His message on earth? There must be something within the bad that we are not aware of. Islam placed pain in the most optimistic light possible when the Prophet reportedly said:

> *Nothing afflicts a Muslim of hardship, nor illness, nor anxiety, nor sorrow, nor harm, nor distress, nor even the pricking of a thorn, but that Allah will expiate his sins by it.*

Mercy is a beautiful gift that comes part and parcel within the pain. But it is only there when we acknowledge it is. And what is more desired to the believer than his Creator's mercy and forgiveness? Knowing this surely eases the believer's pain.

Nietzsche wrote that religion gives hope to the downtrodden, the bullied, the weak, the poor, and the slave. And he is right. The hope that Islam offers is limitless, and that is the point. That is the beauty of Islam and although Nietzsche wrote this as a criticism of religion, it is not a criticism at all. Hope is the most powerful force on earth and faith monopolizes this commodity, of which Islam gives the believer an extraordinary amount of. In Islam, hopelessness is a sin.

The prophets of the past have set a timeless example for us: That even in the most extreme cases of pain, loss, and perceived hopelessness, we must endure the fate that God willed for us, and do it with a positive attitude and remain patient, and be beautiful in our patience. Hopelessness is a sin because it comes from a lack of faith. When you have a robust belief in the power of the Almighty, you always have hope that things will work out, and with a positive attitude, you will overcome it; it's just a matter of time. Allah (swt) backs this up by saying:

*Allah does not burden a soul beyond that it can bear.*

— Quran, 2:286

This verse is God's promise that you can overcome your struggles. To believe in God is to believe in His word, and He communicates to us time and again to stay positive and to have faith in ourselves. All that has come your way is within your capability to surpass. And that is not false hope. It is not one of those statements where you just believe things will be OK for the sole utility of making you less sad. It is an explicit promise made to you by the One who created you and the universe and everything within it. I say this with certainty because this hope is verifiable; just open a Quran.

Acceptance, hope, endurance, and a beautiful patience, and so much more are engulfed within the huge concept of Sabr. It is Sabr that makes us accept what Allah (swt) has decreed upon us. Having Sabr means to not complain about our circumstances because we are fully aware that He is the owner of the universe and that He unequivocally intends good for us, thus His decree is unquestionable, infallible, and complete.

## Gratitude in action

After Allah (swt) split the Red Sea so that Musa and his followers could escape the threat of Pharaoh and his army, they faced a new situation in an unfamiliar land. They were in the middle of a desert, without much water or resources to keep them nourished. They did not have any proper housing to shelter them from the extreme desert heat. They had been traveling, the vast majority of them by foot, for days. Let us recall what Prophet Musa had said to his people that day:

> *And remember that your Lord promised, "If you are thankful, I will give you more, but if you are thankless, My punishment is terrible indeed."*

We might expect him to urge these people who have been through hell to remain patient. This was not the case; instead, Allah (swt) decided it was appropriate for Musa to speak to his followers about gratitude. We learn from Musa's speech to his people to practice gratitude even in times of struggle. Being thankful for the good in our lives helps us get through hard times because it makes us refocus from the bad and toward the good. We can become so caught up in our problems that we forget all the blessings in our lives. Prophet Musa told his people to be thankful when they were tired, thirsty, and without shelter, but still, even they had something to be thankful for. Even after everything they had been through, from living under the brutal oppression of the Pharaoh to being stranded in the desert heat, they exercised gratitude.

One reason why Musa might have urged his people to show gratitude instead of patience is that gratitude leads to patience. In Islam, the two virtues gratitude and patience are closely related. This is because the best way to stay patient, enduring, and persistent is by practicing gratitude. It is hard to be patient without being grateful first.

Some might even argue that the only way to be patient is by being grateful. Because to remain persistent and hopeful when it feels like your whole world is falling apart is difficult without acknowledging at least some things of value in your life. When we take a moment to register the blessings we have been granted in our lives, being patient follows naturally. This helps explain why Musa advised his people on having Shukr (thankfulness) rather than Sabr (patience) when it seems that patience is more appropriate for that setting.


## Giving charity softens the heart


Too often, we attach ourselves to our egos so much that we begin to identify as one with our problems, placing our consciousness in the epicenter of our troubles. We become so immersed in our problems that we forget how good we have it relative to everyone else. We often compare up, with someone who has more than us, and seldomly compare down.

To be clear, no comparison is needed at all because comparing ourselves to someone else ignores our differences. It makes no sense to compare anyone to anyone else when each person has different starting points, goals, and circumstances. Theodore Roosevelt said, "Comparison is the thief of joy," and he was correct. However, acknowledging the fact that some people may have it worse than us can be extremely valuable. Being aware of our position in the hardship hierarchy, so to speak, makes us more compassionate because first, we have to acknowledge other people's pain before we can sympathize with them. It also helps put our troubles in perspective, easing our own pain by making us more appreciative of what we have. Pay attention to how the following quote by Mahatma Gandhi uses perspective to add value to the things we have already:

> *I cried because I had no shoes, then I met a man who had no feet.*

It is obligatory for every Muslim to give charity at least once a year, thus making one shift their focus from their own problems and consider the problems of others. This is important because oftentimes our ego likes to place us in the center of the world, blowing our problems way out of proportion. We have so much emotional attachment to our own problems that we begin to see them being a lot bigger than they actually are, and at the same time making us ignorant of the problems of others. When we take a moment to examine the lives of those not only in our immediate surroundings such as our friends and relatives but also of people all over the world, we develop a more accurate perception of the level of severity of our own struggles.

As of the year 2021, it is estimated that seven hundred million people around the world, most of whom are women and children, are severely undernourished due to a lack of food. Islam forces us to acknowledge realities like this and make us more compassionate toward their suffering. It was recorded that the Prophet Muhammed ﷺ exemplified this level of compassion by saying:

> *He is not a believer whose stomach is filled*
> *while the neighbor to his side goes hungry.*

In this hadith (saying), the Prophet proclaimed that a Muslim is she who is not so concerned about her own well-being that she is blinded to the struggles of her neighbors. She is aware that everyone goes through hard times, and when those around her are struggling, she is making an effort to alleviate their suffering, even if it means giving away her own food.

In a world where resources are finite, generosity, or any act of giving, is a courageous act. It takes courage to give something away, not knowing for certain, whether or not that thing will be replaced. The fear that it won't be replaced comes from a mindset that believes that resources are scarce, which presupposes a lack of faith in the generosity of God. On the other hand, to give without any certainty that that thing will be replaced comes from a mindset of abundance, a tacit trust that God will provide. This is faith, a certain belief in the unseen. Trusting the outcome will be good because He is in total control; this is tawakkul.

In this hadith, the Prophet mentioned one with a "full" stomach, implying that the person has more than enough food for themselves, and possibly enough to share. Nonetheless, to share one's food when you have more than enough is still a noble sacrifice.

The sense of community brought about by helping others causes us to appreciate the good in our lives and the bad that we are lucky enough to call our own because we realize how much worse things can be. Earlier, I introduced a quote by Robin Roberts that said:

> *I bet if we all threw our problems in a huge pile and saw everyone else's, we'd rush to grab ours back.*

I realized late in life that Islam has been teaching this all along. Charity is a central concept in Islam; it is one of the five main pillars. The Islamic teaching creates a sense of global community that places our problems in one big pile, allowing us to not be overwhelmed by our own struggles because we are cognizant of the pains of people all over the world by placing such an importance on charity and compassion. The following story titled "You Brought Me

Dates but You Did Not Remove the Seeds from Them" demonstrates how empathetic we should be.

"You brought me dates but did not remove the seeds from them." Why is this phrase famous and who said it? In the deserts of Arabia centuries ago, a man by the name of Omar Ibn Al-Khattab saw his friend, the Caliph Abu Bakr, exiting the inner city and going toward the village after the *Fajr* (sunrise) prayer. Abu Bakr entered a small house and stayed for hours, then went home. Due to the closeness of their relationship, Omar knew all the good Abu Bakr did except the secret of this house. Days had passed and the caliph still visited this house; Omar still didn't know what his friend was doing inside this home, so Omar decided to enter the house after Abu Bakr came out of it to see what was inside and to find out what his friend did after the Fajr prayer. When Omar entered the small house, he found a destitute old woman who couldn't move. She was blind and had no one to look after her. Ibn Al-Khattab was surprised by what he saw and he wanted to know what Abu Bakr's relationship was with this blind old woman.

Ibn Al-Khattab asked the women: "What does this man (Abu Bakr) do here?"

The old woman replied: "I don't know, this man comes every morning to sweep and clean the house. Then he prepares food for me. And then he leaves without saying a word."

158

Years later, on the day Abu Bakr passed away, Omar remembered the old woman and went to look after her. He cleaned her house just like Abu Bakr used to do. He then prepared her food in the same way.

"Did your friend die?" the woman asked.

"How did you know?" Omar replied.

"You brought me dates and did not remove the seeds from them."

Omar Ibn Al-Khattab collapsed to his knees and his eyes flooded with tears.

The old lady revealed to Omar the level of sincerity the late Abu Bakr, who was motivated by his faith, had when carrying out acts of good. To simply look after a helpless lady is more than enough. To regularly bring her food and clean her house is a praiseworthy act. But to remove the seeds from the fruit before handing them over indicates a deep concern for the comfort of another. And the fact that Abu Bakr did this act in secret shows that his motives were genuine.

Abu Bakr at the time was a caliph, leading the entire nation of Muslims, and to say he was busy is an understatement. But he did not let his status or his own problems get in the way of pitting the dates before serving them to a stranger. His empathetic character shifted the focus from himself and toward others. When we do the same, we put our own struggles in perspective.

This story teaches us many things, but in the interest of this chapter, it shows the internal state of the believer. The believer is one whose heart is soft, whose eyes still tear, and who although may be suffering from their own wounds, still tends to the scars of others. Nowadays we seem to be desensitized to violence; it's as if our hearts have hardened.

Through mass and social media, we are aware of the intensity of global poverty, famine, and violence. The availability of camera phones has made it possible to capture on film imperialist forces terrorizing a people by dropping bombs on their houses or shooting civilians in broad daylight in places like Palestine, Afghanistan, and Iraq. Footage of these atrocities circulates through the Internet and is viewed millions of times by people all over the world. This normalization of suffering can make you feel hopeless in your efforts to help others. It can make you feel like the best of your abilities is barely a drop in the bucket compared to how much suffering there is in the world.

However, Islam tells us that to cause change at the macro level, we must first focus on the micro, namely, ourselves. To do what you can, no matter how small and inconsequential you think it may be, do it anyway. You don't have to build schools or wells to change the world; you can start by offering a smile. All change begins with ourselves, and to change the external world, we must begin by changing our internal state. The famous Islamic scholar and poet Rumi said:

> *Yesterday I was clever, so I wanted to change the world. Today I am wise, so I am changing myself.*

Changing the outer world begins with changing our inner one. One way to change the world is to change your perspective of the world, and the other way is to change it with your own hands just like the story above illustrates.

# 9

# Battle Yourself: The *Nafs* and Higher Self

*"The greatest jihad is to battle the nafs (self),
to fight the evil within yourself."*
—Prophet Muhammed (pbuh)

The most common fear among humans, more common than the fear of death, spiders, or even heights, is the fear of public speaking. That is why I decided to take a public speaking class. I was living in New York City at the time. After I made the decision to turn my life around and reflected deeply on my life, I found that one of my insecurities is having my appearance be judged by others. I spent years living a lifestyle of drugs and partying, feeding into my ego and desires, giving it all it ever wanted. I gave this lifestyle many years of my life and all it gave me was a feeling of emptiness.

Emptiness is the best way I can describe the feeling of looking back at your years and not being able to boast even one achievement. I felt empty because there was a void where the human heart places progress and success.

Along with emptiness I also exited that lifestyle with a whole lot of tattoos. Virtually every inch of skin between my waist, neck, and wrists was inked up. If I were to have you close your eyes and randomly point to an area on my body you would more likely than not point to a tattoo. Having these tattoos meant I would often be judged before I even had a chance to introduce myself. I would come off as a criminal or a threat. Someone who probably wouldn't add value to a conversation. Therefore I was brushed off and avoided.

Even at the local mosque one time in New York, after I had finally mustered up enough confidence to wear short sleeves around my neighborhood, an older gentleman approached me after prayer and admonished me about my tattoos. "Your wudu (ablution) is invalid because the water is prevented from touching your skin by your tattoos," he explained. I was crushed. Although I now know what he said was false, this happened in the early days of my self-transformation, and because I was not very knowledgeable about Islam at the time, I believed what he said.

I developed a case of social anxiety, a fear of being prejudged and overlooked. And I knew immediately that what I feared most, is what I most ought to do. Fear is a terrible state to live in and I had let fear ruin my life for too long. The only way I can master my mind and take control of my life is by leaving my comfort zone. So I signed up for Toastmasters public speaking class.

The public speaking class was psychologically terrifying at first. Speaking in front of strangers is bad enough; speaking about myself in front of strangers felt like mission impossible. Being seen and heard by so many people at the same time meant simultaneously being judged by them, and since at the time I had low confidence in myself and my appearance, negative thoughts kept circling in my head. "They don't even want me here," "My opinion doesn't really matter," I kept saying to myself. To say I was extremely nervous is an understatement. Every time I went up, my body and subconscious co-conspired against me, releasing stress and adrenaline responses. My lower mind knew public speaking was unfamiliar territory and urged me to go back to *safety, comfort.* I stuttered, lost my flow of thought, turned red in the face. My subconscious tried everything to sabotage me, but I did not give in. I was not going to allow my programming to steer my life, not this time.

Every morning when my mind told me not to go to the public speaking class, I silenced those voices and forced myself to get dressed. My mind tried to convince me not to get on the train, not to walk through the building doors, to instead turn back, go home where the outcome is certain and safe. I had to battle myself consciously and strenuously. Every second while I was up in front of the class speaking, a super self-conscious voice would tell me to just "stop and sit down; public speaking is not for me." Despite this, I never acquiesced. It was not easy. It was painful and exhausting but it was worth it. I could not give in to my fear. Author and motivational speaker Jack Canfield said:

*Everything you want is on the other side of fear.*

To overcome your fears is to overcome an unconscious, oftentimes irrational pattern of thinking. And to face fear is to go against your greatest enemy: yourself, the conscious to overcome the subconscious.

Although they have completely different meanings, the mental states of constant comfort-seeking and fear are closely related. To always seek comfort stems from the paralysis of uncertainty. That is being so detached to a predictable outcome that we intensely avoid an unfamiliar experience. When you fear what the future might bring, you seek comfort because comfort is predictable, thus certain. It is in this way that at the very core of comfort, exists fear.

The subconscious longs for comfort, which you must not give it. And through sheer willpower and determination, you must tell yourself that the conscious mind is in control, and actualize your essence. You do this by moving away from the *comfort zone* and into the *danger zone*. Away from predictability and into the *unknown*. Growth takes place in times of discomfort.

This is how you master your subconscious, by forcing yourself to do the things you don't feel comfortable doing.

Since the subconscious operates from the past, doing things that are novel and unfamiliar will feel unnatural and oftentimes painful. The pain is just indicating growth. Just like when you work out in the gym, you first have to put your muscles through mechanical stress for them to grow; similarly, you need to put yourself through uncomfortable situations to master your mind, thus grow. That is exactly what I set out to do when I took the public speaking class.

By facing my fears and forcing myself to get up and speak in front of strangers when every inch of my body was telling me not to, I disciplined my mind, and the more I did it the more I was telling my lower self that I was in charge, and that from now on I will no longer allow my subconscious to rule over me.

Islam is the religion of controlling your desires and through practicing Islam, I learned true self-discipline. The greatest distinction of the human being is that they have been endowed, or some might say burdened, with having free will. Now, how much free will we have is arguable, but at the very least we can all agree that we have some ability to make our own choices.

Having free will and the ability to exercise agency means we are burdened with having to take responsibility for our actions. Animals have an insignificant amount of free will, which is apparent in the fact that they behave with little variability among their own species. Animals are almost completely controlled by the instinctive urges of their biology. That's why we cannot blame a lion for killing the hunter; that's simply its rigid nature. Instead, we question why the hunter put themselves in such a dangerous situation. The Prophet Muhammed illustrates the idea of self-discipline for us by saying:

> *Allah has created angels having reason but with no desires, animals having desires and no reason, and man with both reason and desires. Therefore, if one's reason is stronger than his desires, he is like an angel. On the other hand, if his desires are stronger, he is like an animal.*

We are all inclined to indulge in certain momentary pleasures. And by virtue of being human, we have animalistic urges along with an angelic faculty to control them. Islam does not teach us to ignore our desires or act like they do not exist. Islam teaches me how to balance my desires and instincts by being in control of them, rather than controlled by them.

Being Muslim means to behave in a certain way despite my biological instincts, and in doing so I am practicing self-discipline at a psychological level, and self-purification at the spiritual. This ongoing tug of war between the *nafs*, or the ego, and the *higher self* means that every interaction we have in the world is an opportunity for improvement. Every moment we want to give in to the temptations of our lower selves is an opportunity to empower our higher self.

You cannot help but sense that the nature of the human being, through an Islamic perspective, is dualistic. There seems to be a degree of inherent cognitive dissonance in the human being. It seems that our nature, our temperament, and our character are at odds with our values. We *believe* one thing but are programmed to *act* a different way. This is because being Muslim means acknowledging the division within yourself—the soul and the body.

Islam is not only a belief but a complete way of life. Being a Muslim means committing to actions and refraining from other actions for the sake of God. And devoting yourself to Islam means to submit yourself entirely, your body and soul to God.

Fasting during the month of Ramadan is obligatory for every Muslim who is able to do so. When a Muslim fasts, they do not eat from the crack of dawn to sunset. Eating and drinking are the most basic needs of the human body; if one can refrain from food and water for a long period of time, they have a great level of mastery over themselves, and can refrain from doing almost anything. To not eat and drink is only one part of fasting, as fasting also includes refraining from gossiping, lying, sexual thoughts and acts, lethargy, and many other low forms of behavior. Through fasting, we attain awareness of our bodily needs and a greater awareness of the presence of Allah (swt) and all His provisions. We come to realize the power was always within us to subside our fleeting urges for the greater, eternal purpose.

This concept is what psychologists call *delayed gratification*. Delayed gratification is to set aside your immediate wants for a greater reward in the future. This concept is found throughout Islam. In the case of fasting, the believer's body is intentionally deprived of food and water; despite being hungry and thirsty, they continue to remain patient out of love for the Beloved. They silence their bodily urge to eat because they know of a far greater spiritual reward in the future.

In 1972 psychologist Walter Mischel conducted what is now known as the Stanford marshmallow experiment. In this study, researchers offered young children a reward, either a marshmallow or a pretzel depending on the child's preference. They made a deal, either they received one small but immediate reward, a marshmallow or a pretzel, or two small rewards at a later time. In follow-up studies, the children who were able to control their desire for instant gratification and chose the latter option tended to have better life outcomes as measured by SAT scores, educational attainment, body mass index (BMI), and other life measures.[5] Psychologists have deemed delayed gratification as the utmost reliable indicator for success.

Islam has been teaching delayed gratification since long before any psychologist or motivational speaker. The idea of working hard and remaining patient in the present, for some form of a future reward, is central in Islam. As we have discussed, fasting is a prime example of delayed gratification. So is prayer. A Muslim is obliged to pray five times a day regardless of how busy they are. Whether you are a billionaire businessperson or twenty-something-year-old American collecting unemployment benefits, you are expected to be diligent in all your prayers and to offer them on time.

Let's look at the Fajr, or dawn time, prayer, for example. The believer wakes themselves up at dawn. Dawn time varies every day and depending on which region of the world you live in; however, let's assume on this particular day it is at 4:30 a.m. Not too many people enjoy waking up that early, myself included. Nonetheless, the believer leaves the comfort and warmth of their bed and performs Wudu (ablution). They wash their face with water to wake themselves up and cleanse themselves in preparation for their appointment with their creator. It takes self-discipline to do this and an even greater amount of discipline to do it regularly. There were many times when I wanted to stay in bed knowing I had to perform the Fajr prayer, but I forced myself out of bed. On those successful mornings, my love for the divine overpowered the lethargy of my lower self. On many other days, however, I was not as successful when my lower self had the better of me and I slept through dawn. Sleeping, like eating and drinking, is a bodily function, and when one resists the urge to sleep he or she is exercising the conscious mind to control the body. This is self-discipline in action.

There is a spiritual motivation for doing acts that gain the pleasure of Allah (swt). Prayer, fasting, and giving charity are all done for the sake of God. Ultimately, the goal for every Muslim is to attain the ranks of Jannah, or paradise. "And enter My paradise"(Quran 89:30) are the words every Muslim desires to hear. So the satisfaction the believer gets from thinking about paradise outweighs the discomfort of fasting, praying, giving charity, and all other disciplined acts. The believer controls their desired action for a deferred reward.

Critics may claim that delayed gratification in Islam is a form of barter system and is transactional in nature (I do $x$ in exchange for $y$). Critics may say that there is no real character development of the believer if the only motivation is to receive a reward in return. However, this is a very superficial understanding of faith. While it may be true that part of the motivation for a Muslim is to attain the ranks of Jannah, that is not all. The prime motivator for a believer to fast, pray, give charity, discipline themselves, and exercise all other acts of worship is out of love. I'll leave you with a quote that relieves any concern of a transactional form of worship in Islam.

*O Allah! If I worship You for fear of Hell, burn me in Hell,*
*and if I worship You in hope of Paradise, exclude me from Paradise.*
*But if I worship You for Your Own sake, grudge me not Your everlasting Beauty.*

—Rabia al-Adawiyya

Worship out of a fear of hell is the relationship of a slave to a master. Worship for the goal of heaven is the relationship of a merchant to a customer. Instead, I worship God because He has given me everything. Whenever I have the slightest thought of disobeying Allah (swt), I have an extreme feeling of ingratitude toward all that I have. I worship out of love.

## Meditation in Islam

I first learned about meditation from a secular perspective. I studied the heightened states of consciousness and the power level of focus one can reach by meditating and was instantly drawn to it. I was so obsessed with self-improvement that I meditated for hours on end. I later came to learn that meditation was inherent in Islam.

Islam means to submit or surrender. To surrender yourself, your desires, your actions, and your entire way of life to the will of Allah (swt). The root word of Islam is the Arabic word *salam*, which means "peace," indicating that peace and tranquility come from first surrendering. The entirety of Islam is to be in a peaceful, meditative, and contemplative state. Active meditation in Islam can be broken into three parts. The first is a state of *muraqabah*, or to be conscious of observation. The second is salat, which is a series of prayers performed daily. The frequency of salat serves as proof of the consistent spiritual connection the believer maintains with the divine. And finally, *dhikr*, which is the act of remembering the Creator.

Mindfulness means to be aware of one's own awareness. It means to be conscious of the present moment and all that surrounds you. Its etymological meaning is very similar to the Islamic concept of muraqabah, which comes from the word meaning "to watch or observe something attentively." But in the Islamic version of mindfulness, muraqabah, who is watching who?

Islamic Scholar Muḥammad al-Tuwayjirī defined muraqabah as "the constant knowledge of the servant and conviction in the supervision of the Truth, glory be to Him, over one's outward and inward states." In other words, it is knowing that Allah (swt) is *Al-Aleem* (The All-Knowing), *Al-Baseer* (All Seeing), and *Al-Samee*` (All-Hearing). Thus knowing Allah's (swt) attributes and giving them a sincere and deep place in your heart will help you reach the mindful state of muraqabah.

When you immerse yourself in the reality that your Creator is watching you, you cannot help but become conscious of all your actions and thoughts. You become aware of yourself. You discipline yourself to embody the teachings of Allah (swt). How audacious do you have to be to do something that Allah (swt) forbids knowing He is watching you do it?

In short, muraqabah is a spiritual form of mindfulness where you become more aware of yourself because you know that Allah (swt) is aware of you. When you are conscious and aware of your thoughts and actions, you are in the present moment.

Presence is also cultivated through salat. When a Muslim is praying, he or she is regarded as being directly in front of Allah (swt), reciting the direct word of Allah (swt), and seeking Allah's (swt) mercy and blessings, thus being in a very God-conscious state. This requires a high level of focus and sincere submission to the moment. A deep connection stemming from the heart. Allah (swt) says in the Quran:

> *Certainly will the believers have succeeded:*
> *They who are during their prayer humbly submissive*
> *[khaashi'oon].*
>
> —Quran 23:1–2

The word *khaashi'oon* that is used in this verse comes from the Arabic word *khushoo'*, whose meaning encompasses a combination of the words "concentration," "peace," and "humility" all in one.

The level of concentration practiced in salat has been proven by scientific research to have similar effects in increasing mindfulness and improved overall mental health as seen by secular mindfulness meditation.[6]

The element of humility that is emphasized in salat is what differentiates salat from secular meditation. When Muslims pray, we pray to the one deity worthy of worship. We acknowledge His supreme ownership over the universe and praise him for His perfection. In prayer, a Muslim spends a portion of the prayer in prostration, putting their forehead to the ground, and proclaiming "praise be to my Lord the Most High." The contrast here, the Muslim putting their forehead down to the lowest point while praising the acknowledging the Highest, adequately expresses the level of humility that Islam teaches.

One of the first words said in salat is *Alhamdulillah*, meaning praise and thanks to Allah (swt). Alhamdulillah is then repeated many times throughout the prayer. Salat is an expression of worship but also of gratitude to Allah (swt). When you are performing salat, you are praising the Creator for His provision for all humankind. Modern psychologists and life coaches talk about the importance of expressing some form of gratitude first thing in the morning. Salat is prescribed five times throughout the day, the first one being at dawn, and is often prayed as soon as the Muslim wakes up.

Dhikr is the practice of remembering Allah (swt). It is an act of worship just like salat; however, dhikr is not prescribed at specific times. Instead it is practiced throughout the day. When you ask a Muslim, "How are you?" they will likely reply by saying "Alhamdulillah" first, then tell you how they are.

Another example is when a believer witnesses a wonder of Allah's (swt) creation, such as the beauty of a sunset, the first words that might come to their mind are *Subhan-Allah*, meaning "praise be to God," attributing the beauty of the sunset as a creation of God. These are examples of dhikr done throughout the day.

A person's faith in Islam can be analyzed from two dimensions: internal and external. In the external are the apparent acts of worship such as prayer, fasting, dressing modestly such wearing a hijab, growing a beard, and so on. These are all necessary for establishing a good relationship with Allah (swt); however, Islam is also an internal struggle. It is spiritual development as in for the spirit, the soul. Allah (swt) says in the Quran:

> *Verily, in the remembrance of Allah do hearts find peace.*
>
> —Quran 13:28

The heart and the eternal soul are one. It's what's deep within. Spiritual peace is achieved by remembering Allah (swt). And remembering the Creator is honored through prayer, gratitude, fasting, and the like. However, I found the practice of dhikr to be most rewarding in that respect. The following is a description of dhikr from the famous eleventh-century Muslim theologian Imam al-Ghazzali.

> *Let your heart be in such a state that the existence or non-existence of anything is the same—that is, let there be no dichotomy of positive and negative. Then sit alone in a quiet place, free of any task or preoccupation, be it the reciting of the Qur'an, thinking about its meaning, concern over the dictates of religion, or what you have read in books—let nothing besides God enter the mind. Once you are seated in this manner, start to pronounce with your tongue, "Allah, Allah" keeping your thought on it.*

> *Practice this continuously and without interruption; you will reach a point where the motion of the tongue will cease, and it will appear as if the word just flows from it spontaneously. You go on in this way until every trace of the tongue movement disappears while the heart registers the thought or the idea of the word.*

> *As you continue with this invocation, there will come a time when the word will leave the heart completely. Only the palpable essence or reality of the name will remain, binding itself ineluctably to the heart. Up to this point, everything will have been dependent on your own conscious will; the divine bliss and enlightenment that may follow have nothing to do*

*with your conscious will or choice. What you have done so far is to open the window, as it were. You have laid yourself exposed to what God may breathe upon you, as He has done upon his prophets and saints.*

*If you follow what is said above, you can be sure that the light of Truth will dawn upon your heart.*

Through the practice of dhikr, you are inculcating your internal essence with the light emanating from the divine words of Allah (swt). It is a truly phenomenal experience and develops the believers' mental consciousness and spiritual awareness when practiced often enough.

# Islam transcends the ego

In a hyper-individualized world, we are told that our greatest priority is ourselves. We are told to give in to our pleasures and desires. They say, "you only live once," or YOLO for short, to encourage you to not hesitate in acting out whatever you think might make you feel good in the moment. And for a long time, I conformed to this notion.

When I lived the lifestyle of drugs, money, casual sex, and other pleasures, I lived from my ego. There was no disconnect between the desires that I had and my actions. I acted out every impulse that arose in my mind. If I had an urge to snort cocaine, I automatically acted on that urge. When my body felt the urge to sleep with women, I set out to satisfy that urge. I lived from my ego. The thought of others didn't even cross my mind. I saw the world and everything in it in relation to myself and my own self-interests. Every interaction in the world was an opportunity for me to make myself better off somehow. I needed more money and more pleasure. I wanted a higher status to be praised by others. Satisfying these pleasures was the only standard to guide my moral compass. My only values and principles were those that concerned my ego's whims. And my thoughts, actions, behaviors, and ultimately my reality were steered by my ego.

As I have discussed earlier, living from the ego and for the ego leaves you feeling empty. No matter how much you try to satisfy your selfish desires, they will never feel satisfied. The ego is insatiable. After some time, you can't help but get this extreme feeling of deficiency from within.

This was a sign to me that I am not my body. Clearly, I have a body, but that is not all I am. If I was only flesh and bone, being controlled by a collection of brain cells communicating through neurotransmitters, I would not have had this feeling of emptiness. If I was indeed a solely physical being, bodily pleasure should have brought about a warm feeling of satisfaction and contentment. In fact, the opposite was true.

I was happiest when I deprived my ego. I was most content when I served a cause outside myself. And I was most satisfied when I asserted my higher self over my egotistical whims. The biggest mistake we can make is confusing pleasure for happiness. The ego drags you down the path of comfort, pleasure, and lethargy. You must actively avoid this. Trade in the immediate release of dopamine for the long-term effects of serotonin, even if it means enduring pain and discomfort. Because that is where true happiness is.

I asked myself why so many celebrities who seem to have every material possession imaginable still struggle with depression and mental illnesses? Why is the phrase "money can't buy happiness" so applicable to today's celebrities? It is because money cannot nurture the spiritual dimension of the human being. Oftentimes, having a great deal of money can run contrary to the soul's well-being.

Celebrities, professional athletes, and other high-profile individuals have turned to Islam to provide the spiritual sustenance that their bank accounts couldn't give them. For example, Brooklyn Nets point guard Kyrie Irving embraced Islam in the month of Ramadan in 2021. Irving is someone who makes tens of millions of dollars a year, has a multimillion-dollar sneaker deal with Nike, and has one of the largest fan bases of all NBA players. From a worldly perspective, all his physical and egotistical needs are met. On a superficial level, he was not lacking anything. However, from the inside, Kyrie Irving felt his soul's longing for spiritual guidance such as the one provided by Islam. Kyrie needed Allah (swt).

Kyrie Irving continued to play NBA games while fasting in the month of Ramadan. He performed exceptionally well in those games, oftentimes the highest scoring player on the court as well as dominating other statistics. Irving decided to deprive his body of food and water in an attempt for self-reflection and spiritual purification. He disciplined his body for the sake of his Creator. Irving had all the money he ever wanted. All the cars and jewelry, and was respected for being one of the best basketball players in the history of the NBA, but he realized that all of those worldly ornaments pale in comparison to the eternal riches of spiritual success.

After studying how to reach higher levels of consciousness, detaching from the ego, and attaining self-mastery, I knew that the body is merely a vehicle for the soul.

There was something outside the physical body that needed to be nurtured. That is the soul.

Sociologist Émile Durkheim dubbed the human entity as *Homo duplex*. Human beings are on the one hand biological organisms with animalistic appetites, while at the same time our capacity for complex thinking pushes us to seek something greater than instinctual behavior. We have an innate desire to transcend the shortsighted nature of our egos and devote ourselves to a greater purpose. To me, that greater purpose is Islam.

As a Muslim, every living moment is a moment in the pursuit of transcending my ego. Every time I lower my forehead to the ground, prostrating to Allah (swt) in prayer, I am transcending myself, surrendering to the present moment, and worshipping the Most High. Every second that passes between dawn and sunset during the month of Ramadan that I resist the urge to eat and drink is a conscious endeavor to live outside myself. Whenever I am sacrificing my basic wants, I am prioritizing the unseen over my ego's desires.

## Conclusion

I started this book by writing about what I went through in my past, hoping it would help you to get through what you're going through in your life. I then wrote about how I was able to use those trials as fuel. You must realize that what has happened in the past, has happened. Life goes on, and unless you realize that, you will be stuck in that time and place. Heal yourself, and don't rely on anyone else to do it for you.

This book explains to the reader how I took the initiative to move past what I went through. I put the past behind me and used it as fuel. I imagined all the hurt, the tears, and the emotions as a wall, and put my back against that wall. The only way to go was forward.

Happiness is the ultimate form of success, maybe even the only definition of it. Success is not a fixed place, position, or income bracket. Success is to have a goal and to constantly work toward that goal. Success is a dream, ambition, and discipline. Success is peace. Being content and loving yourself is success.

My intention for writing this book is to show the work I undertook to drag myself toward peace. I hope this message inspires you to do everything you can to move toward your goals. If I can do it, you can too.

The end

# Resources

1.  J. Lutz, A.B. Brühl, H. Scheerer, L. Jäncke, U. Herwig. 2016. "Neural Correlates of Mindful Self-Awareness in Mindfulness Meditators and Meditation-Naïve Subjects Revisited." *Biological Psychology* 119: 21–30, ISSN 0301-0511.
2.  Lazar, S. W., Kerr, C. E., Wasserman, R. H., Gray, J. R., Greve, D. N., Treadway, M. T., McGarvey, M., Quinn, B. T., Dusek, J. A., Benson, H., Rauch, S. L., Moore, C. I., & Fischl, B. 2005. "Meditation Experience Is Associated with Increased Cortical Thickness." *Neuroreport* 16(17): 1893–1897.
3.  Anthis, J. 2019. US Factory Farming Estimates, Sentience Institute, retrieved December 2021.
4.  Petrosus, Elizabeth et al. 2018. "Effects of Orally Administered Cortisol and Norepinephrine on Weanling Piglet Gut Microbial Populations and Salmonella Passage." *Journal of Animal Science* 96,11.
5.  Mischel, Walter; Ebbesen, Ebbe B. 1970. "Attention in Delay of Gratification." *Journal of Personality and Social Psychology* 16(2): 329–337.
6.  Ijaz S, Khalily MT, Ahmad I. 2017. "Mindfulness in Salah Prayer and its Association with Mental Health." *Journal of Religion & Health* 56(6): 2297–2307.

# Other resources

- The Holy Quran, (Eternal)
- Kahneman, D. 2011. *Thinking, Fast and Slow*. Farrar, Straus and Giroux.
- Bukhārī, M. I. 1966. *Sahih Bukhari*.
- Dispenza, J. 2014 *You Are the Placebo: Making Your Mind Matter.*

Made in United States
North Haven, CT
04 August 2022

22283677R00104